ANIMAL RESCUE STORIES

THE COLD, DARK BASEMENT

THE COLD, DARK BASEMENT

ANIMAL RESCUE STORIES
a series

TRUE STORIES OF
ANIMAL RESCUES & INTERVENTIONS

Jodi LeBombard
—Voted National Animal Control Employee of the Year

Parkhurst Brothers Publishers
MARION, MICHIGAN

www.parkhurstbrothers.com

Consumers may order Parkhurst Brothers books from their favorite online or brick-and-mortar booksellers, expecting prompt delivery. Parkhurst Brothers books are distributed to the trade through the Chicago Distribution Center. Trade and library orders may be placed through Ingram Book Company, Baker & Taylor, Follett Library Resources, and other book industry wholesalers. To order from Chicago Distribution Center, phone 1-800-621-2736 or fax to 800-621-8476. Copies of this and other Parkhurst Brothers Publishers titles are available to organizations and corporations for purchase in quantity by contacting the Special Sales Department at our home office location, listed on our website. Manuscript submission guidelines for this publishing company are available at our website.

Printed in the United States of America

First Edition, July 2024

Printing History: 2027 2026 2025 2024 12 11 10 9 8 7 6 5 4 3 2 1

Library Cataloging Data:
Series: Animal Rescue Stories (vol. 1)
1. Canine rescue practices
2. Bovine animal rescue
3. Public policy-animal abuse and rescue
4. Author: Jodi LeBombard-Animal shelter work experience

ISBN: Trade Paperback 978-1-62491-206-1
ISBN: e-book 978-1-62491-207-8

Parkhurst Brothers Publishers believes that the free and open exchange of ideas is essential for maintaining our freedoms. We support the First Amendment of the United States Constitution and encourage all citizens to study all sides of public policy questions, making up their minds.

Cover and interior design by Susan Harring Book Design
Acquired for Parkhurst Brothers Publishers and edited by Ted Parkhurst

0724

Dedication

This book is dedicated to my mother and father who supported my every move in life, guiding me and backing me to reach my goals. I never would have had the opportunities I've had without them.

And to my Lola dog, who taught me unconditional compassion and filled twelve years of my life with love, getting into the trash, going broke buying ham bones, refusing to share with the random homeless animals I fostered, and jumping in my side of the bed with muddy paws. I guarantee Lola, AKA Trixie, is being *wayyy* overfed cookies from my father in heaven right now.

Preface

Growing up in a desolate area on over a hundred acres of land in the middle of nowhere, Michigan's Upper Peninsula gave me ample opportunity to foster and rescue quite a few animals. Somehow, I managed to find stray feral kittens and sneak them into my room without my mom knowing right away. I would find injured wildlife and try to help them get better (although this was almost never a success). I remember one dog that really started my drive to save animals. There were dogs that I fostered and dogs that my family took in for one reason or another, but this one dog stole my heart and started my desire to want to save as many more as I could. I obtained the dog from a local woman who devoted her life to rescuing animals in need. In order to keep up, she needed foster homes to help her care for the animals. This one day, I had to have been about thirteen, she brought me a dog that "needed a lot of work". It was a yellow shepherd lab mix named Baby. She dropped off the dog, and it was a mess. It was skin and bones and wouldn't come near anyone—nearly feral. When she handed me the leash it was frantically pulling away, trying to get away from me. She told us the owners had kept it chained to a tree on a heavy tow chain for years with almost no human interaction. The dog was petrified and wouldn't come near me. We too, had to chain it up at first. Our dogs would just free-roam outside. Since we lived so far back in the woods, there was really nowhere for them to run off to. It took me days of feeding this dog, sitting near it, and telling her it was going to be ok before she would *almost* approach me. After several days, I saw a change in her behavior. She wagged her tail when she saw me, and her eyes told me she trusted me. It's an unexplainable feeling you just have to experience to understand.

This was the day I unhooked her chain, looked into her eyes, and said, "Be free." The dog instantly took off faster than I had ever seen a dog run. I instantly had an "oh shit" feeling come over me, questioning myself if I misread her trust since she was running away. I stood in the yard as she ran and disappeared on the other side of the house. I never expected what happened next. She came around the opposite side of the house running full speed. She continued running and running in circles around the yard and house before running full speed up to me, jumping up as if she wanted to give me a giant hug. It was an immediate, unforgettable bond that made me feel that this was my calling. Over the next few weeks, I never had to chain that dog up again. She free-roamed with the other dogs all day and went into our finished two-car garage with the other dogs to sleep at night; that way, they wouldn't mingle with coyotes. I will never forget this dog. Every night, when I called her and the others into the garage for bed, she would hug me and not let go. I've never had a dog do that before. She would jump up and almost wrap her legs around me, not letting go. I would have to almost peel her off me and run every night to get out of there. The bond I had with that dog was unforgettable. I knew the animals in this world needed someone like me to be their voice—to stand up for them.

Several years later, I must have been about twenty-two years old, I was sitting at my job caring for individuals with mental illnesses and reading the local newspaper with them. This was one of two college jobs I had. I had my very first dog by my side, whom I adopted from the local humane society. I would bring her to work with me every day to visit with the patients. College had kept me in the big city. I enjoyed my job so much with these individuals—they were like family—but I knew it wasn't what life had prepared for me. With a father as a retired police officer and a mother as a state investigator, law enforcement was in my blood. What with my equal love for animals and law enforcement, I always wanted to be an animal control officer. I had my mind made up from a very young age. That is when I came across a job posting for a county animal control officer. I was super excited but knew it was a long shot with all the competition I was sure to be up against. That night, I submitted my resume and hoped for the best. A week or two passed and to my surprise, I actually got a phone call asking if I would like to come in for an interview. I was ecstatic. I went shopping for a new outfit, spent hours getting ready, and showed up over an hour early, driving around the block over and over, waiting to go in without being *too* early. I remember the interview being in the conference room at the animal shelter. An officer, the director, and a deputy director sat across the table from me, asking about my experience with animals. I went on about all the animals I rescued in the wilderness during my childhood, my passion for the job, and my schooling. I walked out of the interview feeling like it went pretty well. I made the interview panel laugh several times, but I still wasn't sure that was enough to push me on top of all the other applicants, who I am sure had a lot more on their resume than spending years petting and rescuing random animals. A couple of weeks went by, and I did not get a phone call. I was losing hope and suspected I wasn't the one chosen. But then one day, I was sitting at my second job—my full-time job—working with juvenile delinquents, when I got a phone call. I remember I was working in the control room that day. I pretty much sat behind glass opening doors, communicating over a speaker to the staff and youth. I felt like I was in a dream. I was offered the position, and of course, I accepted. I remember being so excited when I hung up the phone that I jumped up and down and hugged my supervisor at the juvenile facility. Neither one of us was the hugging type, but I couldn't help it with how excited I was. I felt like I had just won the lottery.

My first year on the job was spent responding to general animal control calls of service—dogs running loose, dog bites, vicious dogs, general welfare concerns of animals, and so on. With my love for animals, I began taking a special interest in the animal welfare complaints. I struggled a bit being so young and inexperienced with real city folks, not the easy-going country-living people I was used to, but quite honestly, I think my easy-going trustfulness gained me a lot of street credit. I wasn't what these people were used to. I listened, I was respectful, and I genuinely gave a shit. The cruelty, neglect, and dog fighting cases were exciting and rewarding to investigate. In each and every case I was assigned, I fought for the animal to the fullest. You would regularly see me at the state crime lab dropping off evidence and at the prosecutor's office handing over felony warrant requests for the animal abusers in the county. I left no stone unturned in my investigations, and my cases rarely went cold. I wouldn't just take the animals from abusers—I would watch over them at the shelter and make sure they found a good, loving home. My director at the time saw my drive to save these animals in neglectful or cruel situations and created an animal cruelty position at my department, which I applied for and was awarded. I owe her a lot for recognizing my talent and putting me in a position to use it. I hit the ground running.

I've been pouring my heart and sole into my job for well over a decade now. Between working full-time and then some, pursuing my bachelor's degree in criminal justice, and tending to the many animals that I took under my wing, the last several years have been life-changing. The joy and the heartache have left me with experiences no animal lover could ever imagine. I have seen some of the worst things imaginable done to animals, yet some of the most moving and touching things people do to help save them.

I am writing this book for many different reasons. At the least, I want to change the negative "dog catcher" stereotype that many people still think of when they hear "animal control officer." We are not all big bad dog snatchers that roughly throw animals in a cage for euthanasia. I want to educate the public and encourage people to speak up and report animal cruelty and neglect—don't turn your head to it. Animals need you to make that phone call for them. And I want you to get a glimpse of what is really going on in the community around you—something I never would have imagined was so prevalent until I began my career as an animal cruelty investigator. Lastly, I can't support my dream of having acres of land, full of rescue animals to live out their lives spoiled rotten, on my measly animal control salary.

Contents

CHAPTER ONE

Holy Cow

When you work in animal control, one of the things you realize pretty quickly is there are many different opinions about how animals should be treated. You have the parka dog people—these are people who believe dogs should be outfitted in a parka before they step foot outside on a cold day. You have others who think that real dogs live outside in a straw-filled shelter. Some people think of their dogs and cats as their children. Some think of them as companions, but not exactly part of the family. Others will have animals for the sole purpose of working or doing a job for them—guarding livestock or the property, hunting, or providing a service. To each their own, as long as they provide adequate food, water, shelter, and veterinary care and are doing what is best for their animal. At the end of the day however, regardless of my opinion, I have to enforce the law, not my own personal beliefs.

As a person who looked at animals as indoor, fleece jacket-wearing pets, it was hard to put aside my personal beliefs and keep an open mind when I started this job. Even more so, I had minimal education on livestock—only what I knew from growing up with my sister and her horse. Through education—learning animal breeds, watching and studying them, and gaining experience of my own—and investigating countless animal neglect and cruelty cases day in and day out, I now have a vastly different understanding of animals.

For example, I once put a dog coat I had at the shelter from a case on a newborn baby goat because it wasn't having the easiest time flourishing. Once I had put the dog coat on the baby goat, it was like the mom wanted nothing to do with her kid. Having a hard time understanding why the mom was acting this way, I consulted with an expert on goats who told me the problem was me. I caused it by putting the coat on the goat. Sure enough, the second I took that coat off, the mom returned to nurturing her kid. Little things like that taught me you actually *can* kill animals with kindness. It's actually not cool to feed your pets so much that they become obese and can hardly get around. In my opinion, that's almost comparable to not feeding them enough. It's about the individual animal, the breed, the environment, and the age—all these things go into what's best for the animal.

When people think of animal control, they seem to only think of picking up stray dogs and cats. While this is sometimes the case, it's far more than that. That's one of my reasons for writing this book. I want people to know what animal control does behind the scenes. My county was a big city with rural areas as well.

My dispatcher came over the radio, calling out my badge number. I heard my dispatcher say, "The caller wants to make a complaint about a neighbor's loose cow in the roadway." It was a Saturday, with only me and one other animal control officer covering the entire county. Our county consisted of well over 280,000 people, and the animal control dispatch phone lines sometimes rang off the hook with residents calling in complaints. Although I primarily only handled the cruelty and neglect investigations, I would just run call-to-call on Saturdays. With only two officers on the road compared to the usual five or six on a given day, it was hard to keep up without me working the routine calls too.

Before I even had a chance to punch the address into my truck computer, I recognized the crossroads of where the cow was reported to be as they dispatched me over the radio. It was near a farm that was known for its cows getting out. I had never been the officer sent out there, but I recognized it from hearing the other officers routinely being dispatched out there for this. It was one of those addresses we were always being sent to: always about loose cows, always writing the owner tickets and telling him to fix his fence. I thought to myself, a little annoyed, *Here we go again with this person,* and felt motivated to get to the bottom of it.

I pulled into the driveway of the neighbor who had called in to report the cow in the roadway. It was standard practice to stop at the complainant's house first unless they specifically asked us not to. He came out looking furious, for which I didn't blame him. "I can't tell you how many times I have called about this," he said. "The Sheriff deputies come out, and you guys come out, and no one ever does anything! You tell him to fix his fence, but he doesn't!"

I stood patiently listening to him, nodding to affirm his complaints. I didn't take it personally. He just needed someone to hear him and do what his taxpayer dollars should be doing. So, despite my hectic day, I listened to him talk in circles and vent. He pointed to the deep hoof prints that led through his well-kept lawn all the way to the road and a few cows out loose grazing at their leisure in the field behind his house. Then he pointed out the farmhouse next door where the cows were from and reiterated how much he had just HAD IT with these cows getting out. He said it wasn't a couple of times; it had been a steady issue for years. "Years! I've been calling in this complaint for years!" he added.

I wrapped up the conversation and assured him I would get to the bottom of it. I honestly didn't blame him for his irritation with the situation; I would be irritated, too. I was honestly kind of irritated with this cow owner after I heard all this neighbor had to deal with. To start, I found it odd when I glanced over an acre or two from the neighbor's to the cow owner's farm but didn't see any cows when I was told he had quite a few. Furthermore, I noticed that the acreage surrounding the farm was being used for growing corn and other crops—no pasture. It was hard to see entirely since everything around the old farmhouse and barn was grown up and unkempt.

When I train new officers, I always encourage them to check the welfare of livestock if they are out loose. Welfare means the food, water, and shelter situation. I have this rule of thumb: almost all horses, cows, etc., are not interested in getting loose if they are content with their surroundings. If you picture livestock out in a field, what do they like to do? Meander and eat, graze, and graze some more. This isn't always the case, of course. There are some unruly horses and cows, but comfort does seem to play a role more often than not.

I jumped back in my animal control truck and headed down to the man's house where the cows live. I caught up with the cow owner outside in the front yard. He was quite old and hard of hearing with his age. He looked like the stereotypical old-time farmer. He clearly hadn't showered in several days. His face was so covered in dirt it was tinted black when it was white. He was clearly wearing the same flannel and jeans that he would throw on each day without washing. It was just him that lived there, no one else. I started as I always did, introducing myself and explaining why I had been called to his house. We talked about his cows being out and that he'd need to get them back in.

"Yeah, I'll go get the tractor to round them up," he said as if he'd had numerous times in the past. Before he got onto his tractor, I hollered to him, "So where's the rest of your herd?" I truly didn't see cows anywhere. The old man pointed to the old, run-down barn and said they were behind it. His hearing was so bad I had to yell, and even that sometimes wasn't loud enough. Maybe the guy next door got a kick out of it, thinking I was over there yelling at him. The house on the property was old and dilapidated. The lawn was overgrown. The barn area wasn't clearly visible between the broken-down farm equipment strewn about and all the brush. "Before you go round up those cows, let's take a look at your fencing back there," I yelled to him. He turned around, slowly walking toward the barn as if for me to follow him. It took a good few minutes through the trail of overgrown yard, brush, and junk on the property to get out to the back of the barn to see the cows.

As I rounded the corner of the barn to the cows, my jaw must have nearly hit the ground. I couldn't fathom what I was seeing. There were about forty cows in a small area about the size of two city lots, about a quarter-acre. Some panels were lined up together as a fence, but also just old farm equipment: a broken-down wagon, tractor attachments, and such, stacked in a circular pattern to keep the cows in. The cows stood there mooing, as if to say, "Help us *please*." They were all standing in deep, deep manure. It was about six inches deep in some places, others a few feet at least.

In the deeper area, I noticed one cow was not moving. It was in the standing position but so deep in the manure that its belly was touching the ground and its head laid out in front of it. Several of the other cows were standing around it nearby. I realized it was dead within seconds of me taking a better look. I asked the old man what happened to that cow, and he replied nonchalantly that it got stuck in the mud a few days ago and couldn't get out, so it eventually died. I was nearly speechless and irate with the conditions of the cows as I looked around further, but I kept my cool with the old man. That's professionalism, as taught to future animal control officers. This was one of the many cases that would test the line between my professional and personal beliefs.

I continued to look around. There wasn't a speck of hay anywhere in the confinement area. The cows were acting starved. They were mooing frantically and moving toward me as if they were demanding food. If you've ever spent time with cows, you know the moo when they are demanding food versus the moos to say hello. I noticed a round bale of hay off in the distance, outside the pen, where the cows couldn't reach. I asked the old man where the water trough was, and he pointed to the other side of the pen. I couldn't be sure there was water in it from where I was standing, so I proceeded to head in that direction with the old man. As I got closer to the water trough, I began to see through all the other cows. There was another dead cow lying near the water trough, with all the other cows standing by it.

"What happened to this cow?" Growing more furious but somehow managing to keep my composure, I asked, "How did he die?"

"Well…when I threw hay into them, they all ate it up before that one could get any, so I think it starved to death."

I couldn't believe his nonchalant tone. He had known the cow wasn't getting food but had done nothing.

I had already radioed for my partner the minute I saw the deplorable conditions. I asked him to drop what he was doing and come back me up because this was a terrible situation, and I would not be leaving until I had a plan in place to get these cows out of here, fed, and humanely housed. These weren't dogs, so I couldn't just put them in my truck to seize them. A livestock seizure requires a search warrant, a livestock trailer for hauling, somewhere to take them, and a whole lot more.

"I need you to get some hay into this area," I told the owner, as we waited for my partner to arrive.

"Well, now, I don't have a tractor attachment to move it into the area," he said.

"Ok, I guess we're bringing it to them by hand," I replied as I began to work.

We carried armfuls of hay at a time in the almost unbearable heat. Between my partner, the old man, and myself, we fed the cows. The cows were attacking the hay and pushing each other out of the way, frantically trying to get some hay. We didn't stop until I knew each and every cow had a decent-sized meal.

My partner was usually a big prankster. He was also an officer who wasn't necessarily there for the animals. Still, his ambition to be a police officer made him take his job as an animal control officer seriously when we were in situations like this one. When I heard him holler my name from a distance and saw him motion for me to come by him, I could tell it wasn't good. As I approached, he pointed to an almost lifeless calf lying in the corner all by itself, unable to lift its head. I rushed over and assessed the calf, which I quickly determined was in critical condition. I was beyond furious at the old man now, but again, I somehow kept it together.

"What happened to this calf?" I asked the landowner.

"I think that was its mother that died," he said as he pointed to the dead cow stuck in the mud. "I guess I should have given it a bottle or something."

I looked at that old man, saying nothing but making a promise in my head that I would make sure from this point forward that he would never own a cow again in his life.

I picked up the baby calf and could feel its every rib. It would try to lift its head, but it would just fall back limp. I told my partner I was leaving to transport this calf to the local university for help, and that I would return shortly.

My body was exhausted from the wear of the long day, moving armfuls of hay, and the overwhelming heat, but I knew I had to get this calf to my truck. Trudging through the manure with the calf in my arms, I could feel my muscles shaking—ready to give—but I knew I could not let go of him. I pushed through, telling myself over and over that I was almost there. And just when I didn't think I could hold on any longer, I reached the truck.

I put the calf down on a blanket in the back. I felt like I'd never be able to lift my arms again. Speeding off to the local university, I called them on the way to let them know what I was bringing in so they could be prepared.

We finally reached the hospital, and when I went to the back of the truck to get the calf out, I hoped and prayed as I opened the door that he would not be dead already.

He wasn't. He had a chance. I carried the calf in and stayed with him for a few minutes while they hooked him up to machines and stuck a tube down his throat—emergency procedures. I had to leave the calf there and return to the farm. I knew he was in good hands.

Upon my return, countless other discoveries of neglectful and cruel behavior were made. Several more cows were discovered dead around the property. There was a cow with nearly the whole side of its face infected and a large hole through her jaw. We later determined it to have been an untreated abscessed tooth that ruptured, and the infection had continued to spread. As the discoveries continued, I concluded that this was by far one of the worst cow cruelty cases I've ever witnessed.

I pursued felony animal cruelty charges for the old man, and within days, he was charged and received orders from the judge that he was not to own or possess another cow for a very long time. The cows had been removed from the property, and miraculously, the university saved the calf that was nearly dead when I handed it to them. The university didn't stop there. They fell in love with the calf and took it in, locating it a loving forever home where it continues to live the life it deserves.

Cow with a hole in its face and infection eating away at the side of the face.

Dead cow lying outside of the pen.

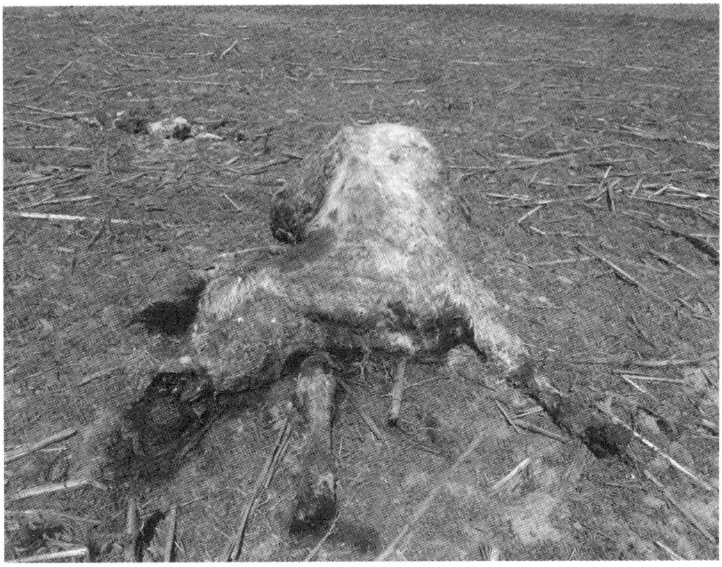

Dead cow with dead calf nearby decomposing in the field behind the pen.

Dead cow decomposing in the barn.

CHAPTER TWO

Dino the Loving Lab

Dispatch radioed my badge number, followed by an address in the city. I was being dispatched to a neighborhood in a less-than-great part of the city. Dispatch advised it was a landlord calling in, wanting animal control to respond to his rental house. I wasn't far away and was familiar with the area. The butterflies in my stomach told me this wasn't anything good. Whenever a landlord called, the situation was usually grim. I radioed back to dispatch, "Ten-four, got it." I would head over.

As I pulled up to the address in my animal control truck, I saw the landlord sitting in his truck outside the house, awaiting my arrival. The house was your typical city rental, a basic house with old siding and windows, just decent enough to do the job. The yard was kept up, but there were no flowers and no sense of home added to the yard.

I radioed back to dispatch that I had arrived and quickly jotted down my arrival time and the address on my daily log. Switching on my handheld radio, I jumped out of my truck. The landlord and I met at the sidewalk in front of the house. We began meandering towards the house as we talked. I introduced myself, and he began to tell me the issue. He told me how the residents had been evicted days ago and showed me the eviction paperwork. They had taken all their belongings and moved out even before the final eviction papers were posted. Now, with the house empty and the eviction date passed, he sent his cleaning crew to the house to get it back in order to rent it to the next tenants.

The cleaning crew went into the house this morning and, to their surprise, were greeted by a dog that was left behind inside the house. The landlord went on to tell me the cleaning crew put the dog in the basement with a bowl of water. He commented that the owner hadn't had the decency to even leave the dog with any food or water. We continued to walk and talk as we made our way through the empty house, and then he pointed to the basement door. It was a typical city rental in this neighborhood, smelling of stale cigarettes and left disrespected.

I've been to countless places like this for similar problems. It was almost always an aggressive pit bull on the other side of the door, secretly just scared and thinking it was supposed to be protecting its house. I carefully cracked open the door to size up what I was working with this time. When you do this job for as long as I have, you can learn a lot from how a dog will react by spending even ten seconds saying "hi" to it. If the dog is cowering and barking, they can usually be won over with some time and trust. If the dog's hair is raised, and its tail is pointed straight back, not so much. An assessment of the dog's behavior is always the first step. This tells you what tools you'll need to handle the situation safely for everyone involved, including the dog.

As the door cracked open, I placed my boot in front of the door in case the dog charged. That way, the door couldn't be jolted out of my hand. That's another thing. Although the cleaning crew was able to place the dog in the basement, the dogs almost always act much different when a shiny badge and uniform comes towards them with an authoritative demeanor. But not this time. To my surprise, out poked a black nose, eager to get the heck out of the basement. I could see the shadow of a black body wiggling back and forth with excitement. A tail was banging back and forth off the wall with anticipation, so thankful and happy to see someone. A huge sense of relief came over me when I realized I wouldn't have to resort to my catch pole (snare) or tranquilizer gun. All I had to do was grab my disposable slip leash out of my cargo pocket and loop it around his neck as he struggled to blow past me out of the lonely, scary basement. As he emerged from the basement, what I saw was the opposite of an aggressive pit bull. He was the sweetest little happy-go-lucky black Labrador.

As I looked at the dog, my heart went out to him. I

could count every rib in his body. It must have been days since he had last eaten. Even if he had dined with his owners, they hadn't fed him enough. That poor, sweet soul didn't hold humans responsible, though. He was oblivious that his owners had cared for him so poorly, intentionally leaving him behind. Instead, he frolicked about, so thankful and eager to please, wanting to know if I would be his best friend. We headed for the door to leave, and I thanked the landlord for calling to get him help. I jotted down the landlord's name and contact information as a witness while the dog pulled and wiggled, so excited to get out of there. The landlord could give me the owners' names from his eviction paperwork.

The owners would be facing animal abandonment charges. If I couldn't find them, they would eventually be found by the police once a warrant was entered into the computer system. Now, I needed to document the abuse. I typed up my police report and photographed the scene and the animal as evidence. Once my report is completed, it goes to the county prosecutor's office for review. If they feel the elements of a crime are present—that they can prove who did what and when—they issue a warrant. It's up to me to take the warrant to the judge for signature and enter it into the computer system. The next time they have police contact, and their name is run through the law-enforcement system, *to jail they go* until they can see the judge.

We went out to the animal control truck. I unlocked the big back door and opened it up, inviting my new furry friend to jump in. I always kept excessively fuzzy beds and blankets back there for the animals. Some old-timers I worked with would throw a towel down and call it a day, but not me. My co-workers would joke that the cages I set up for the animals when I dropped them off at the shelter looked like a Sears portrait studio with all the blankets and decorations. Then there were the times I would break the rules by letting the dogs sit in my back seat, stopping around the corner to put them in the back of the truck so when I pulled up, my boss wouldn't notice.

It was about a twenty-minute drive back to the animal shelter from this part of town. Dino (what I later named the black lab) and I got back to the animal shelter towards the end of my shift for the day. I swiped my card to enter the gated back area of the shelter to unload him. As I opened the back door of my truck to retrieve him from the ride, he was just so excited to be with his new friend again. I walked him around outside for a minute, letting him get some fresh air. He couldn't have been any happier; his tail couldn't stop wagging.

Dino walked with me as I carried my gear into my office for the day. I couldn't lock him in a cage after all he had been through. Our next stop was the animal food storage room, where the tasty, canned dog food was kept. That's another thing the shelter staff hated me for. I overfed the animals all the time. Why would they care? Because lots of food turns into lots of feces. They always came in to find poop-filled cages when I worked. As a matter of fact, I would play popcorn with the dogs in the cages before I left at night. They *loved* it. Popcorn is a game I made up. You take a giant barrel of those dog treats that are almost like cheese puffs and walk down the row, tossing a handful over the top into each cage. The dogs can't get enough of it, searching all over their cages for the treats. I poured a can of dog food into a bowl for Dino, and he scarfed it down within seconds. I wanted to give him more and more, but giving a starved dog too much food can actually do more harm than good. Numerous small meals throughout the day were what he needed to get him back to a healthy weight.

Dino and I went to the exam room, where I ran him through the intake process. He got his picture taken, his weight recorded, an identification tag zip-tied on his dog collar with his shelter animal number, and all his vaccinations. The next stop would be into a dog kennel. I just couldn't do that yet. I couldn't lock him away by himself to wait for someone to come for him again. Instead, I let Dino come with me into my office while I began typing up my warrant request report for his owners. On the afternoon shift, at the end of the day, I could do stuff like this because no one was at the animal shelter but me and the dispatcher. Everyone else had gone home for the day. As I sat in front of the computer typing away, I felt him slowly sneaking his front paws onto my lap, and he hid his head under my arms while I typed. What a sweet boy. Eventually, he lay down on the floor next to me, tail flapping up and down every time he heard a noise. I glanced down at him, wondering to myself how his owners could leave him behind, not knowing if anyone would ever find him before he starved to death. How could someone be so cruel? It saddened me to think of him sitting in that vacant house, likely staring out of the window, patiently waiting for his owners to return, not knowing that they had left him to, quite possibly, die.

I grew so attached to Dino over the next couple of days, often stopping in to check on him in his kennel, that I let my emotions get the best of me. I let down my walls, the walls that you need to have to an extent to do this job, and felt that he deserved better than sitting in a kennel and waiting for the day he would be adopted. I brought Dino home with me and fostered him until he eventually found the loving home he deserved. My own dogs and cat at home just rolled their eyes when we walked in, like *Oh, here comes another project we have to deal with.* Dino, as you can guess, gained *a lot* of weight at my house. His new owner was the opposite of his previous ones, an active jogger looking for a best friend and jogging partner to run with him daily. Dino couldn't have lucked out more.

Dino on the left. At my house in foster care with my dog Lola weeks later.

CHAPTER THREE

A Sad Day for a Walk in the Park

Every year, like clockwork, a complaint gets called in when the circus is in town. There are always concerns about the treatment of the circus animals, and I don't mind going and checking on them. Minimally, it's good to make an appearance so the circus knows we are monitoring their well-being. Furthermore, it's not every day that you get to go behind the scenes and stand inches from tigers, elephants, camels, you name it. At the same time, it's sad to see them pacing around locked away in a cage or chained up. On this day, one of the elephants stuck out its trunk like a curious little kid checking out my boots and uniform; cute.

As I was leaving the circus, I got word that one of the

other animal control officers had been sent out on a complaint for a dead dog in a crate that was left in a local city park. It was beyond cold out since it was mid-January—freezing cold, probably about twenty degrees. Immediately, I thought the worst, but hoped there was some reasonable explanation for a dead, frozen dog locked in a crate to be dumped in the park. As it was a possible animal cruelty case, I was called to assist in the investigation.

A short while later I met up with the animal control officer. He showed me the dog, lying on his side, stiff and dead, in a small plastic kennel. He was a male pit bull. The sides of the kennel were smeared with the soupy fecal/urine material that had pooled and frozen at the bottom of the cage as if he had thrashed around before death. There was over an inch of this fecal/urine material at the bottom of the cage with the dog frozen into it. It was sickening and hurtful to see this poor dog lying there as if he died helplessly in misery. I knelt and whispered to that dog, "Don't worry, buddy." I promised I would do everything I possibly could to find out what happened to him and put someone in jail for his inexcusable death.

Canvassing the neighborhood with photos of the dog proved unsuccessful. No one knew anything about this dog or seemed to have ever seen him before. My director had posted the flyer on the animal control Facebook page, hoping to get the word out and get someone to recognize the dog. Shortly thereafter, the local media got ahold of the picture. It was aired on the local news stations, asking the public to come forward with any information on this dog. Our phones and tip line provided countless tips and information, but nothing held true. The tips were often just neighbors who hadn't seen another neighbor's similar-looking pit bull in a while, etc. I would go out and verify the neighbor's dog was alive and healthy, then move on to the next tip. Nothing was turning up any real promising leads. I looked at the case repeatedly, telling myself there had to be another way to find this person.

Suddenly, a light clicked on in my head. There was a small UPC barcode sticker on the crate with the name of the chain pet store where it came from. There was only one of these chain pet stores in the area, the next being a half an hour away. It was a stretch, but what if I took the newer-looking collar and plastic crate to the local chain pet stores and, somehow, tried to find out who purchased them? If they used a credit card or something, I could trace it back to them. It was a long shot, but it was all I had to work with.

My hopes grew as I arrived at the pet store. I had the store workers call for a manager to help me out. I explained what I was trying to do, showed him the specific crate, and provided the UPC numbers. I couldn't have gotten a more motivated person to help solve this: the manager was a huge dog lover, eager to see this person rot behind bars. He disappeared into his office for a good twenty minutes. I didn't know how he'd spent all that time, but when he returned, he had some excellent news followed by some bad news. He pinpointed the exact date and time of the transaction, but the customer had paid in cash. It wasn't over, though. The customer had applied for a rewards card with the store, which means they filled out the application with their name, address, and everything I needed just a few weeks prior. The manager went on to explain the process, saying the application would have been mailed to their corporate office, likely sitting in the mail room waiting to be processed. This dog-loving manager didn't stop there. He had already contacted the head of the corporate office, who just so happened to be an even bigger dog lover and who apparently instructed the employees there to begin sifting through the massive pile of applications until it was found. Awesome! I left the store excited that I had such a strong lead and waited for the phone call from the manager with the information.

Meanwhile, our victim dog had been transported to the local university for a necropsy to find out the case of death. The devastating results came back as a mixture of freezing to death along with inadequate food and water. That poor dog! I couldn't wait to hold someone responsible for this tragic set of events.

When I got the phone call from the manager, my hopes were demolished. The suspect signed up and got the rewards card but didn't fill out the information on the application as they should have. I was left at a dead end again. I sat down and was rethinking my next move when the dog-loving pet store manager called back with some promising news, just what I needed to proceed with the investigation. The person who owned the rewards card had made a return of a cat toy or something of that nature. Per the pet store policy, when someone returns an item, they must show their ID, and the store must document their information. I now had my name and an address. Was it a coincidence that the address was just houses away from the park where the dog was left? I thought not. Furthermore, there were drag marks in the snow from the center of the park where the dog kennel was left, all the way to the edge of the park, pointing toward that exact house.

When it appeared no one was at the house, I went to all the homes surrounding my target house asking for information, but no one had much of anything to tell since the house was a rental and the tenants moved in just a month or so prior. None of the neighbors had paid attention to whether the last tenants had a dog.

My next move consisted of contacting the city code compliance department for information on the house's owner since all rentals have to be documented with the name, and contact information of the homeowner, etc. This was perfect, as the owner of the house turned out to be a fairly big rental company which had a local office. I went right down to their office and explained my intentions and the circumstances. The staff there was enthusiastic about helping solve my problem.

Yes, more dog lovers! They pulled the rental agreement, and there it was, my next piece of supportive evidence. A signed rental agreement from the renters affirming that they owned a dog that matched the description of the dead dog exactly. The name from the pet store matched the name on the rental agreement; it was a boyfriend and girlfriend living there. The rental office had even more information for me though. Apparently, when the suspects/renters first moved in, they had two dogs but only wrote the one down on the lease. They were told that the rental company would be doing an inspection thirty days later, and if they still had two dogs, they would have to pay a second pet deposit. It just so happened that the thirty days had been up just a few days before this. The rental office went on to say they had followed through with this and had called to set up the inspection, but the boyfriend said the dog had gotten sick, and he gave it away. Perfect! Another piece of supportive evidence. We were closing in, but I still needed enough evidence in the courtroom to prove this beyond a reasonable doubt.

I had another idea. I called the manager at the pet store and asked him what kind of surveillance equipment they had in the store, and what the chances were of me getting a copy of my suspect purchasing the collar and plastic kennel. It turned out that this pet store had some of the highest quality, up-to-date surveillance you could get. I requested copies of the purchase videos and had them in hand a week later.

Meanwhile, I found out where the suspect's girlfriend worked and went to question her. She ended up telling me way more than she should have. She completely threw her boyfriend under the bus, providing me with a written statement that her boyfriend did own two dogs and kept them in the garage twenty-four-seven. She went on to tell me he recently purchased a kennel to separate the two since they were reaching nine to ten months, and one was a female, the other a male. She claimed she never dealt with the dogs, cared for them, and rarely saw them. Next, she went on to say she had received a text message about a week prior that the male dog had died (just a day before the dog was found in the park), and he didn't know what to do with the body, "But that was all he told me," she said. I felt deep down that she was just as guilty. What kind of person sits in their heated house, knowing that two dogs are shivering out in the freezing cold garage, knowing full well that they could freeze to death, but does nothing to care for them? The girlfriend was just as guilty in my book, but that would be up to the prosecutor to decide.

My investigation was solid at this point, but why not make it overwhelmingly solid? After obtaining a search warrant for the house and garage, I discovered dog items and evidence to support my case further. There was even an outlined pattern on the garage floor where the plastic kennel had sat. Further investigation led to the second dog, alive and well, living with someone the boyfriend had given it to.

I was ready to call my suspect and break the bad news that a warrant would soon be out for his arrest. He answered the phone, and I explained who I was, saying that I wanted to meet up with him to talk about a dead dog found in the park. He danced around, saying he didn't know anything about that and that he had never owned a dog. I stopped for a second and started over politely but confidently, telling him I knew it was his dog. I went on rambling, "I have you on video surveillance buying the kennel it was found in, I have a lease agreement signed by you saying you own this dog, I have a very credible witness that says this was your dog, the drag marks in the snow lead to your house, do I need to continue, and there isn't a jury in the world that would believe this wasn't your dog."

I then asked him if he wanted to take this opportunity to tell me the truth about what he did to his dog, even though I already knew, or if he wished his statement in my report to be the lie he had just tried telling. The next words out of his mouth mumbled *lawyer* and I replied, "Yes, a lawyer would be a good idea," and I politely ended the conversation. I knew I would sleep well tonight; he, on the other hand, wouldn't.

CHAPTER FOUR

The Love of a Man for His Cats

I was frantically typing my prosecution reports at the animal shelter in my office and as usual, I was backed up trying to fit hours of work in with only minutes to spare. My dispatcher asked me if I could go help the police with some cats since everyone else was tied up on other emergency calls. She briefly said someone had died, and the police were waiting for us on the scene to come pick up two cats. Ugh, this was one of the calls that just broke your heart. It is so sad to pick up animals when their owner has died. The animals are always so traumatized, wondering what is going on and where they are going, questioning why some stranger is taking them from their familiar house and where their mom or dad might be. It's devastating that you can't tell them what happened and reassure them that it is going to be okay. I do so anyway, but they just don't get it, human-feline communication being what it is. But this call was much worse; I had no idea what I was about to walk into.

I arrived on the scene and was greeted by the police officer standing by. He proceeded to tell me to be prepared when I go into the house. Confused, I looked at him and asked, "Be prepared?" He replied, "Yes, the owner has been dead in the house for at least a month, and the smell is overwhelming." He went on to say the ambulance had not arrived yet, so the deceased man's body remained in the house.

I mentally prepared myself as I approached the door and walked in with the officer. As I stepped into the house, the odor of death was pungent and overwhelming. I glanced around to see several huge bowls filled with cat food. One was empty, but there had to have been enough food in the other bowls to last the two cats for another month or longer. *This is odd,* I thought to myself. The officer went on to fill me in on the heartbreaking story. He said the owner completed suicide. They found an unopened letter addressed to the owner that he had written to himself. It was a letter explaining he had two cats and wanted nothing but good for them. He went on to tell their names, their ages, and a little history of each one. His word-for-word request was, "Please make sure my cats go to a good home, not to the animal control shelter." This just broke my heart. This guy committed suicide and left out enough food for his cats, so he knew they would be fine for months if no one found him. I knew I couldn't honor his request not to take them to the shelter, but I promised him in heaven that it would only be temporary. I would check on them daily and make for damn sure they found good homes.

The first cat had beautiful green eyes. She meowed and walked up to me, so sweet, as if she was happy to see a friend. I put her in a cat carrier to transport her. I began looking around the house for the other cat. As I walked through the house, I saw an abundance of plants throughout the house. Once beautiful, they were now dead and dreary. I looked all over the house for the second cat, which according to the deceased's note, was black, the hardest color cat to find when they don't want to be found. I looked behind tables and under furniture, in the cupboards, everywhere, but found nothing.

The last places I hadn't checked were the owner's bedroom (where the owner's body was) and the basement. The door to the basement was closed, but the police officer assured me it was closed when they arrived, that the cat couldn't be down there. That meant I had to check the owner's bedroom. Ugh, I really didn't want to have to see him. I see enough heart-wrenching things that I try to turn my head when I can to keep myself mentally sound. This time, I had no choice. I had to check the deceased's bedroom, where I figured the scared little cat would be hiding.

I stood in the doorway, telling my mind to go away and not remember what I was about to see. There he lay in his bed, dead and somewhat decomposed. The covers were pulled up as if he had taken an overdose of pills, went to bed, and never woke up. His small TV was still playing, and his bedside lamp remained on from the night he chose to take his life. I entered the room and looked all over for the cat. Under the bed, behind and under the dressers, but again, nothing.

I grew worried this other cat hadn't made it because his note said it was around thirteen years old. I wondered if it had curled itself up somewhere inconspicuous and passed away. After looking in every possible spot with the police helping, and spending a substantial amount of time doing so, I had to consider that I did all I could for now. But I wasn't satisfied with not finding this cat. My gut told me it was somewhere in the house. Could it have run outside unnoticed when the police were going in and out? Could the owner have given it away between the time he wrote the note and the time he took his life? It's possible, but I couldn't give up on this cat. It must be somewhere in the house, I concluded.

I talked to the police officer, voicing my concern the second cat was likely still in the house somewhere. Resorting to my experience, I knew that, in the past, setting a live trap had always been highly successful. The police officer agreed to wait for me while I drove back to the shelter to get one since the ambulance and other things were still in the works. I took the cat in the carrier back with me. She rode up front with me in the truck, and I told her what a good girl she was for the whole ride. She purred the entire way back as I talked to her. When we arrived at the shelter, I put that cat in a cage with a big cuddly blanket and told her everything would be okay soon.

Now, back at the house with the large live trap, I baited it with some really stinky cat food. (You cat owners know how they love smelly food!) I left it by the sliding glass door so I could come back throughout the day and check on it without bothering the police to unsecure the house and let me back in repeatedly. I picked up all the cat food bowls from the floor and locked them in the bathroom, leaving my livetrap as the only food source. I walked away from the scene, hoping this was the solution to locate this poor cat.

As for the cats, I told my director about the poor man's wish in hopes that she would get a plea out to the appropriate foster home contacts or something to ensure they (still hoping I would discover the second cat) get into a good home as soon as possible. She was always good when it came to these situations. She has a big heart, too. I also told the staff about what this cat had been through, so they could give her extra hugs throughout the day and make her extra comfortable until a home could be located.

I persistently returned to the house to check my live trap every few hours throughout the day and into the next day, but no cat and no signs of a cat were evident anywhere. I would glance around outside while I was there, and I even had a couple of neighbors watching out for the black cat, too. At the beginning of the third day, I knew my live trap would not work and that something wasn't right. Either the cat was not there in the first place, it was dead, or something was wrong. I contacted the police officer who had a key to the house, and they agreed to meet me over there to get my live trap out. The police officer who showed up was very kind and seemed just as concerned about finding the cat as I was. She unlocked the door, and we went in to get the trap. She was very understanding, allowing me extra time to look around again, and even jumped right in to help. Between the two of us, we looked absolutely everywhere in the house but still came up empty-handed.

The basement door remained closed, and I told her that the initial responding officers said it was closed when they came, and no cat was down there. We both looked at each other like, *Yeah, we want to look anyway* because this wasn't making sense. The basement was dark and dreary, so we pulled out our flashlights to get a good look under shelves and in dark corners. We were calling out to the cat while looking, but still nothing. I thought, *Maybe it just isn't here. Maybe I need to accept that this cat is not here.*

Suddenly, the police officer and I saw eyes flash when we swept some shelving with our flashlights. There it was, a black cat! I was so relieved. I gently pulled out the cat and cuddled it the best I could while wearing my hard bulletproof vest under my uniform, which doesn't make me very cuddly. The cat was terrified and likely dehydrated and hungry. I was honestly a bit irate that I was told the basement door was shut when they arrived and not to even bother checking down there, but at the same time, I was just grateful the cat was found and safe. There was no food or water in the basement left out by the owner, so I knew he hadn't locked it down here a month ago because it wouldn't be alive. I knew the door got shut when officers arrived at the scene, but that's beside the point. All was well.

Back to the shelter we went, and gosh, was I thankful I put in the extra effort. The thought of that cat dying down there if I had given up hope made my stomach knot. When we arrived at the shelter, I made sure we said *hi* to the cat's sister, who seemed happy to see the black cat. They were adopted into loving homes before we knew it.

CHAPTER FIVE

The Possessed Cat

It was a busy day as usual, and my list of places to get to consisted of a long itinerary. Surely I would only be able to get to half of it! Just before I began, my boss called and asked me to go on a "Special assignment really quickly," and he chuckled. I thought, *Oh, here we go. What could it be this time?* And *Surely it is never "really quick,"* as I laughed to myself. He rambled off an address and something about me needing to pick up this lady's mean cat.

I arrived at the house in a small, out-of-the-city town. It sat on a dead end and overlooked a creek. It was peaceful and quiet at the home. I parked my truck and headed up to the door, where I was greeted by an elderly lady whose facial expression told me she was glad I'd arrived. A look of relief on her face was my reward for making the extra stop on this busy morning. When I walked into the kitchen with her, her house was quiet—almost morose.

I asked her about the cat in the basement, and why she needed me to pick it up, etc. She had a dreadful look on her face, a look of hurt and pain to think about it. The lady went on to tell me that she had owned the cat for about seven years now. A couple of months ago, her husband passed away, and it was mainly his cat. About a week ago, the cat began acting strange, hissing and being mean to her. She kept elaborating on how it was just the weirdest thing and wasn't making any sense to her. She explained she thought if you just gave the cat some time, it would pass, but it didn't; it continued to worsen. With a fearful look of desperation, she went on to say the cat had now begun to go after her, acting extremely vicious, like it was "possessed," chasing her around the house and trying to attack her.

The lady said the day prior she had to get a card table with the legs folded up to use as a barrier between herself and the cat just to get it downstairs and locked in a bedroom with its food, water, and litter box. She had contacted her veterinarian, but she couldn't even get near the cat to take it to the vet's office without it trying to attack her. She went on for several more minutes about how absolutely vicious and possessed the cat was acting. She cautioned me repeatedly about the care I needed to exercise when I got down there. At this point, I was growing a bit concerned by her sincere fear. The lady told me she had stacked a bunch of heavy books in front of the door to the room the cat was in since the door wouldn't latch the day before. The books were weighty, but somehow, the cat threw itself against the door and snuck out, requiring the owner to get her cat back in the bedroom again.

The lady didn't dare accompany me downstairs when I was ready to get the cat. She was clearly freaked out, and I didn't blame her. I could see in her eyes it was also tough on her, as it was her now-deceased husband's cat, for the most part, too. Losing him and now facing this must have been tough. As I crept down the stairs, she hollered how careful I needed to be a couple more times. I will not lie; my heart was racing, and I was somewhat laughing at myself for how ridiculous it was that I was this nervous over a cat. In my defense, I had never dealt with an attacking cat before!

Once in the basement, I was getting even more freaked out. It was an indescribably eerie feeling down there—even worse than when I walked in the front door. I felt like I was in a horror movie, in the ultimate scene. Encountering the door with all the heavy books stacked up in front of it, I seriously considered calling for backup. The only reason I didn't call was that I knew I would be laughed at for that one. I approached the door and slowly cracked it open. There was the cat sitting right in front of the door, looking at me as if it was possessed by a demon. It made a menacing, extended hiss and growl sound, and pissed a puddle of urine where it sat. I shut the door, thinking, *holy shit, are you kidding me?* I whipped out my cell phone, planning to call my boss and ask him why the hell he always gets me into these crazy things... But to my surprise, I had no service! Even creepier! I was in an area that should surely have service. After I walked back upstairs, I told the lady I needed to get a few more things from my truck. I must have grabbed nearly every tool in my truck, including my dog snare and some tranquilizer with a pole stick. I walked back by her carrying all these tools, and she must have thought, *What the hell is this lady doing?* But I wasn't messing around with this cat. Not a chance.

Plan one, I was going to crack open the door and attempt to use my dog snare to hold the cat and get it into a carrier. Of course, when I opened the door, it was nowhere to be found. *Shit,* I thought to myself, *I am going to need to go into the room with it.* Plan two, I loaded up my pole syringe with enough tranquilizer to completely knock out the cat. With a snare in one hand and drugs in another, I went in. I was slowly creeping around the room, looking for the cat. The thought crossed my mind that I was being "punked" or something, but I wasn't. That lady probably heard my knees knocking in fear all the way upstairs. There were shelves of canned goods and storage items all over this room. About five minutes later, I located the cat. It was hiding behind some canned goods and peering through an opening at me. I crossed my fingers, and half closed my eyes before I quickly gave it a poke of tranquilizer with my pole syringe, and then ran out like a total wuss until the drug could take effect.

There is no real kicker to end this story. The cat simply

fell asleep as a result of the tranquilizer, and I brought it back to the shelter as the owner requested. Immediately upon my return, I hunted down my boss to tell him the story. He found it quite amusing, poking at me in good fun as I told the tale.

CHAPTER SIX

Buttons and Jacob

When I first began this job, I took animals home with me *all* the time. I've had so many cats and dogs spend the night, it's ridiculous. As time went on, I slowed down on this. I was becoming too overwhelmed with seeing the terrible things I saw at work all day, every day, and then coming home to take care of my own dogs and cat, amongst whatever other furry friends I had visiting that day. These animals, of course, wore on my house, too. Cats reaching up and sharpening their claws on my leather couch ends, and dogs chewing on my coffee table when I left the room. I remember one hound dog that shit all over my floor when I was at work, ran through the feces multiple times, then jumped up on my door to smear it in over and over as he panicked that I left him home alone. He certainly had some separation anxiety going on.

My own animals were tolerant to the revolving door of misfits but weren't all that happy sharing all the time. Although I struggled to leave the sad, pitiful faces at the animal shelter in a cold cement-floored cage, I slowly backed out of overwhelming myself and began only taking a dog or cat home here or there when one really touched my heart. I would take home the emaciated dog (skin and bones), the dog that needed to be fed small amounts every hour, or the cat that had an upper respiratory infection so bad from the stressful shelter environment, it was facing euthanasia—things of that nature.

I ended up making it through that chaotic phase of my career with only one foster failure (a dog I brought home with the intent to only foster, resulting in falling in love, and adopting instead), a goofy basset hound that I love to pieces. Well, that was the case up until Buttons and Jacob.

• • •

When I come in to work for the day, I am typically handed a stack of "complaints" from residents wanting to file various grievances, such as a neighbor's dog running loose, or that they were bit by a dog when out jogging, or commonly anonymous welfare complaints. As an animal cruelty investigator, my assignments are primarily welfare-type concerns.

This day, I left the locker room fully dressed in my bulletproof vest, shined-up boots, uniform, and pinned-on badge. I made my way from the locker room, down the shelter hallway, into the dispatch office, pulling my radio off the charger and sliding it into my gear belt. The dispatcher was usually eager to hand me a stack of complaints. We were always backed up, it seemed, and they would get a lot of grief from residents calling in wanting us there right that second. The dispatcher would have to field those angry calls when we were running behind (overwhelmed).

I briefly glanced through the stack of complaints I was assigned for the day, making a game plan on what seemed pressing and what area to head out to first. One of the calls read "anonymous" as the caller just said, "sheep tangled up," and the address where this was located. I assumed this meant, well, maybe some sheep got tangled in something, and the owner wasn't home to untangle them. Picturing sheep tangled up, I bumped this call to the top of my list and out the back door to my animal control truck I headed.

I checked the lights on my truck, did a quick walk-around to make sure everything was secure, and jumped in to start it up after securing my shotgun in the middle holster. I reached down and called out my badge number, leaving the animal shelter and advising dispatch I was clearing the animal shelter en route to check on the sheep. This address wasn't super far from the animal shelter, which was located just outside the big city in a rural town. It was a ten-minute drive to the sheep but on a pretty busy, heavily traveled county road.

I knew I was getting closer to the addresses based on the numbers I passed; I rarely used my GPS. I knew where the zero delineator roads were and all the main roads. The delineator road is where the house numbers start at zero and grow from there either north, south, west, or east of the road. You could drop me anywhere in the county and I would know exactly where I was—and how to get to the next place. It's just something you learn when you respond to addresses day in and day out for years. Drop me in a different county, and that wouldn't be the case.

I was driving down the road, passing by mailboxes looking for my address, slowing down as I got closer—there it was. I pulled into the driveway. The house was out in the country perhaps twenty miles from the city, but still with neighbors a few acres apart. The driveway was long, and the handsome house was set back from the highway. I didn't think much as far as welfare or neglect of the sheep. I was thinking, *These people obviously take very good care of this expensive house.* Almost always, when a home is well-maintained, the animals are conscientiously looked after.

My guard was down. I was relaxed, looking for these sheep so I could untangle them from whatever they'd gotten into, and call the owner to let them know what happened. That would have been a usual procedure. My mind was thinking a few steps ahead about all the other calls I needed to get to once I handled this quickly.

Expecting the owner was probably at work or something and wouldn't answer the door, I knocked anyway out of courtesy before I would go tromping around someone's yard looking for tangled sheep that I didn't notice anywhere when pulling up. To my surprise, the owner came out of the house and greeted me. He was of a different nationality but spoke English well. Still confused about what the issue was at this address, I introduced myself and asked him if he had some sheep somewhere on the property and if they were okay since we had a caller saying they may not be.

The owner replied, saying he did have some sheep, and yeah, they were just fine.

Being the snoopy, "I don't believe anyone until I see it," animal cruelty investigator I am, I asked him where they were and told him that I just needed to take a quick look at them to verify everything was okay so I could document that I did so in my report. He turned to throw on his shoes, agreeing to show me. He stepped outside, and I began following him around the large house toward the backyard.

As we rounded the house, I saw a circular twenty-by-twenty-foot pen off in the distance with several young sheep and a goat in it. The pen was quite interesting. It was a large round pen made from that white PVC-type material with fencing attached to it. It certainly wasn't the sturdiest looking pen, and you could tell the sheep and goats kind of pushed it around the mowed yard, grazing while still being inside. The weather outside was hot, very hot; over ninety degrees, maybe closer to one hundred. I first noticed they didn't have any water inside the pen and absolutely no shade out in the open field backyard. A couple of the sheep were lying down. We got closer, and I was still puzzled about them "being tangled."

When we got right up to the pen, I began making small

talk with the owner, buying myself some time to get a good look at the sheep without appearing to be too intrusive. He went on to tell me that he got them a while back and was raising them for the meat. They weren't even a year old. As we were talking back and forth, I noticed something tied around their legs. Again, trying to avoid a "Get the hell off my property!" response and be cool with the guy, I looked closer and nonchalantly asked him what was with the legs having ties around them. The owner explained as if it was just another day, that they kept getting out of the pen. Frustrated, he inquired with a relative back in his home country who told him to hobble them so they couldn't jump out or stray far. Instead of hobbling them with actual hobbles that you would buy at the store or order online for the purpose of humane temporary restraint (while milking or something of that sort), he found some heavy-duty coat hanger-type wire, and wrapped it around their legs, running it from one back leg to the other back leg, then from one front leg to the other front leg so they could only waddle or hop around—literally tying their legs together with a heavy-duty wire.

This just didn't sit right with me. Hobbling with actual hobbles intended for temporarily restraining a milking cow or getting a horse to chill out is one thing, but this wasn't that. I wasn't okay with him using this heavy-duty coat hanger material to keep them all tied up twenty-four-seven. That's the scenario that ran through my mind as I assessed the heavy wire "shackles."

While standing there, getting my bearings, with all of

the new information I'd gleaned so far, I dealt with being completely unprepared for something this inhumane. Meanwhile, the guy went on to tell me how this same relative he asked for advice from told him to just "break their legs" and lay them in the grass, moving them every once in a while so they could graze although they were immobile.

I kept an even-keeled posture with my poker face, just nodding my head. "Oh, that is so interesting," I casually replied. Inside, I was alarmed and thinking, *What the actual hell!?*

This guy went on to tell me how he didn't *actually* do that, though, because he felt that was cruel.

"You think?" I thought to myself!

Still small-talking, the owner told me how that same relative told him that once the legs correct themselves and they are able to walk again, the sheep will be dependent upon the owner and won't stray anymore. I kept my cool and just continued the conversation as if I wasn't fuming inside with disgust from what he just told me.

While standing by the pen discussing this and the lack of water, shade, etc., more or less easing into the fact that this whole scenario was not okay on multiple levels, something caught my attention. Flies were buzzing around, but not all over them, just attacking the legs near the hobbles. I knew exactly what that meant: open wounds and infections. I instructed the owner to get into the pen and bring me over one of the sheep to take a look at. He complied, stepping over the PVC makeshift pen and scooping up one of the sheep to hand over the fence to me. When I knelt down and more closely inspected the coat hanger hobbles, I was appalled at what I saw.

He must have put these coat hanger hobbles on weeks, or even a month prior. Since the sheep and goat were younger, they were growing. Those hobbles had grown right into their legs—they were completely ingrown to the point that it hurt me to see it. The wires were actually disappearing in their legs as their bodies grew around them. For some of them it wasn't as bad as others.

I instructed him to immediately start removing the wires from their legs. This was worse than I thought, and my mind was already made up—these sheep were coming with me, not remaining in his care. This was well beyond education. This was cruelty—intentional. He and I removed what we could, but I was going to need a veterinarian to more than likely surgically finish taking off some of the rest with some pain management medication.

It was time to be direct with the owner. I could brook no more dancing around this—I told the owner that I was going to transport all the sheep to a veterinarian immediately and instructed him to hand me one sheep at a time. I honestly and confidently told him, without any emotionally fueled threats, that those sheep were suffering in pain, and they'd be going with me. The long walk from the pen back up to my truck in the driveway seemed like miles in the hundred-degree weather. I was dripping with sweat carrying them the lengthy distance from the back all the way through the yard and out to my truck in the drive. But the hundred-degree weather when wearing my bulletproof vest with my uniform and boots didn't compare to what these sheep must have been feeling with ingrown coat hangers in their legs. Flies had laid eggs (turning into maggots) in their infections, and they had no shelter or water in this heat. As I loaded up the last of them, shutting and locking the back door of my topper on the back of the truck, I told the owner that I would be following up with him to further discuss the situation. I jumped back in my truck and radioed that I had multiple sheep on board en route back to the animal shelter.

The county is not exactly a huge goat, sheep, or horse-type area. They are around, but it is not common at all that we seize them. So, as I began traveling down the road away from the house, I thought to myself mayyyyybe I should give my boss a forewarning that I just did this. At the same time, I was chuckling to myself, imagining he was going to reply with, "You did what?!"

I called him and broke the news, "Ummm, well, you see, I kind of just took a bunch of sheep from someone, and they are really bad, and I need to take them to a live-stock vet… Now."

He replied "They are really bahhhdd (making a sheep baying noise)?" and started laughing.

I yelled at him, saying, "This isn't funny, they are really bad," and then, "Ok, haha… Maybe that was a good one, but for real, I need to take them to the vet." He was support-ive, of course. My boss and I always got along great and had a good time at work. I stopped in at the shelter to give all the sheep some water. Then, I proceeded on my way, driving my charges to the local livestock vet at the university. It was just too hot not to give them a breather from the back of my truck and offer them some much-needed water since I wasn't sure when the last time it was that they had any.

While at the shelter, I carefully removed some more of the coat hanger hobbles from some of the sheep that hadn't had them removed yet. Doing so, I got an exceptionally clear view of the damage to their legs, which was extensive and just disgusting. The hobbles had grown right through the tendons. In some, the wire was fused to their leg bones. I felt terrible for these sheep. A couple didn't even want to stand up, or maybe couldn't. We loaded back up and went right to the large animal hospital. After dropping them off, knowing they would be hospitalized for at least a couple of days, I never saw them again. The hospital took such great care of them and even volunteered one of their well-respected vet techs to foster them.

The next day I returned to the owner's house to explain the extent of the injuries, and how I would be pursuing criminal charges for the cruelty and neglect. While at his residence I ended up picking up the goat as well. The goat was never hobbled, but we don't leave animals on the property of someone who is facing cruelty charges; we take them all. Whether an offender is allowed to keep *any animals* is left up to the prosecutor and defense attorney to hash out, and the judge to decide a disposition.

When telling the owner that I would be picking up

the goat as well, I asked him if he had any others on the property. He was surprisingly honest and led me to a field where he had one more sheep. This sheep had also been hobbled, and the owner hadn't taken its wires out from the day prior when I picked up the rest of them, and he saw how bad it was. In addition to still having the metal wire around his legs, he was tied to a cinder block in the middle of the hot field. He was lying down because he could barely stand. I carried him to the truck, feeling so terrible for him. I hadn't seen him yesterday because I'm sure he was unable to stand then, too.

Instead of transporting this goat and sheep to the veterinary hospital, I brought these two right to the shelter since our shelter veterinarian was in that day. I tucked the goat away in a nice outdoor dog run with some straw for bedding, hay to munch on, and a large bucket of water. Meanwhile, the sheep just lay in the veterinarian's room as our veterinarian cleaned his wounds, wrapped his legs, and started him on some medications. I took the poor sheep outside afterward. He would try to walk but then fall because his legs and tendons were so damaged.

Over the course of the next couple of months, we awaited the process and a court date. The goat and sheep spent weeks at the shelter. I would take them out of their pen every night after my shift and let them graze on the grass and play around. They were very funny. Jacob (the sheep) with his splinted and wrapped legs that worked much better now, and Buttons (the goat) would run around and get into everything. During this time, we all became attached to each other. It got to the point that I would let them out of their cage, and they would just follow me around the facility like shadows. I was working the evening/night shift at this time. The shelter would be closed, so I would walk up to my office where I typed reports in the evening, and they would be right behind me, hobbling along, trying to keep up. I would sit there and type reports while they stared at me and nibbled on my keys and things on my gear belt. I fell in love with these two clowns. They were quite the pair of best friends.

Buttons and Jacob ended up going into a foster home the shelter director had found a short while before the court date. I found myself missing my buddies every day. The foster parent didn't intend to adopt them; she was just a nice lady giving them a place to be until we decided what we would do with them after a court disposition. I would stop by her house every now and again to drop off fresh wraps for Jake's legs or whatever she needed for them. They would get so excited to see me, it made me miss them even more. I made up my mind one day that I was going to see if my dogs would tolerate these clowns moving into our backyard. I had a small basic house on the edge of town. It wasn't in the city, but it wasn't totally in the country, either, and I had a pretty spacious backyard that was entirely fenced.

In my off time, I went out and built a large pen, and cut a dog door in the side of my garage. So, the goat and sheep had a nice pen with a doggy door to go inside the garage for shelter. When I brought them home, my dogs walked out in the backyard, took one look at them, and looked at me as if, "You have got to be shitting me, really, Mom." They got along just fine. The little goat and sheep ended up growing into a big goat and sheep. Buttons turned out to be 180 pounds full grown, and over a few months I spent a small fortune getting them the best of everything: scratchers, hay feeders, coats for all seasons. I even sweet-talked some cable installers into giving them a giant, couple hundred-pound spool to horse around on in the backyard. I think this was the turning point when my sister began calling my house "The Funny Farm."

The owner, in this case, was criminally charged, and the court ordered him not to own animals for a period of time. So much for stopping by to untangle a sheep really quickly.

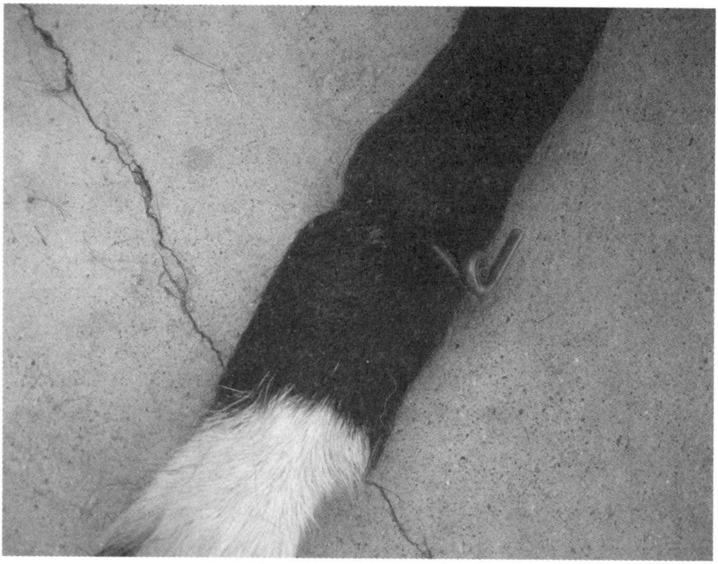

A sheep's leg with the wire still attached.

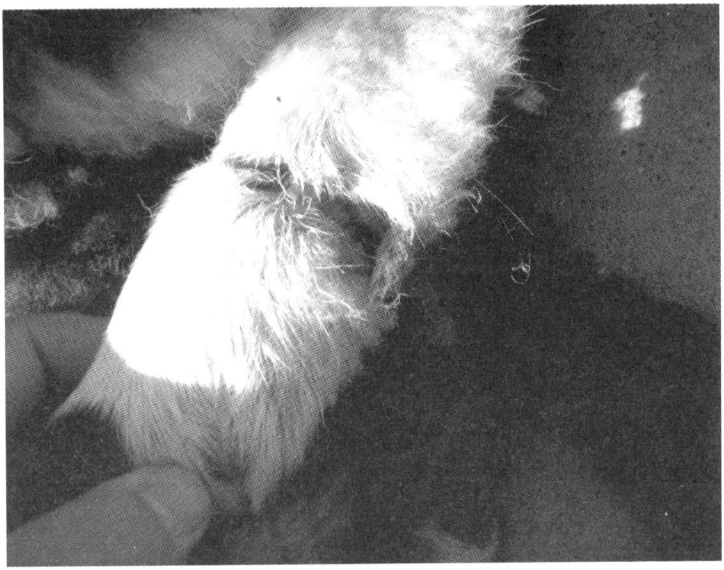

A sheep's leg after the wire was removed.

One of the sheep healing in foster care.

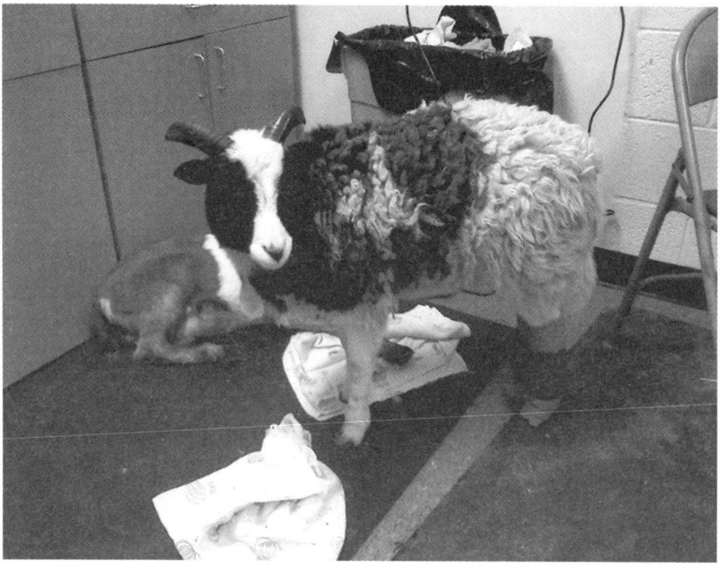

Jacob at the animal shelter getting his legs assessed by the veterinarian.

CHAPTER SEVEN

Shane and a Rainy Dreary Day

It was a dreary rainy day. It had been raining and pouring for hours. It was summertime, and our calls were coming in one after another, as I've mentioned they commonly do in the summer months. We could barely keep up. Our dispatcher was stressed out, and the other officers on duty were running call-to-call. The radio chatter hardly let up. Clear here, arrived here, set this for a follow up—nonstop radio noise. I was working the afternoon shift that day, coming in mid-day, and working until nighttime. I suited up and rushed right out onto the road as soon as I checked in, with the intent of busting my butt to keep us afloat with all the people calling in. We had people reporting, "I have been attacked by a dog," or the police calling because they are waiting on the side of the road for us to come get a dog out of a car because they just arrested the owner and are ordering a tow truck for the vehicle. You name it, it was happening. All high-priority calls, all at the same time.

One of the other officers had been dispatched to an abandoned cat call out in the country hours earlier, but he hadn't made it yet since other calls that were more pressing kept trumping his ability to go there to check it out. He'd get rerouted to help the police with something or rerouted to a vicious dog, loose and actively attacking people, or a dog hit by a car and lying injured on the side of the road. That officer was morning shift, and it was now getting close to the end of his day. Dispatch radioed to him they were reassigning the call to me, and to disregard it on his end. After all, I was not too far from it as I left the shelter. The shelter was just outside the city, with the country being in the opposite direction of the city. The shelter was pretty much the midway point between the two. This call was in the southeast area of the county.

The only information I had been given was of a person who resides in the country area who had witnessed a red truck driving by, slow down, and the driver throwing something which they thought may have been a cat out the window and driving off. The person who called in to report it had not been able to read the truck's license plate number nor give a description of the driver. I had nothing to go on other than a red truck. Bummed about that since I knew there was probably no way we could hold the person who did this responsible, I headed out anyhow, expecting this cat may be long gone by now.

The person who called in told our dispatcher that when they saw this happen, they walked out of their house to see what it was and confirmed it was an orange cat. The caller further told my dispatcher they didn't want to touch it or do anything with it because they were concerned it could be diseased or something (give me a break). I was a little irritated by this since it was pouring rain, but at the same time, I told myself that *at least they picked up the phone to call the shelter and get help for the poor cat.*

It had now been hours since the person originally called to report this. Without a whole lot of hope that I'd even find the cat, I continued on and rounded the corner on the road where the cat was said to be. Creeping down the road, watching the mailboxes for house numbers, I was approaching the house whose owner had reported the incident. It was still raining heavily, which made it relatively difficult to see through my windshield wipers which were whacking back and forth at full speed. I took it slow, searching, scanning the roads, sides of the roads, and—as well as I could—peering into the ditches. Now, a couple of houses away from where the cat was supposed to be, I slowed way down, figuring I would pull over once I got in front of the house and look through the ditches and the surrounding area for this cat. Suddenly I noticed a blob on the side of the road. As I approached, I thought to myself, *It couldn't be?!*

It was. It had been hours since this happened. It

was pouring rain and had been for all those hours. But to my surprise, there was the cat, sitting on the side of the road like it hadn't moved since it was thrown out. It was drenched and looked pitiful. I felt beyond terrible for this poor cat. I jumped out of my truck and scooped it up into my coat. It was completely dripping wet. We ran back to my truck and jumped in. I was relieved to be out of the downpour. Looking down at this poor cat, I saw that it was almost motionless, probably in shock, having given up on help. I apologized to the poor thing that we had taken so long to arrive. I checked it over the best I could and found skin skidded off in areas and gravel ingrained into it, likely from when it hit the gravel on the side of the road. Again, this poor cat was in shock. I knew the only option was to take it immediately to a veterinarian.

The cat rode in my coat, cuddled up and trying to dry the whole way there. The veterinarian didn't find any broken bones, just a lot of road rash, a broken heart, and something very disheartening. His tongue was severed almost completely through. The veterinarian suspected the cat bit its tongue as it tumbled down the roadside. She opened his mouth and showed me. Midway back, his tongue was sliced across about three-quarters of the way. My heart went out to the poor little cat. Then I said what we say on a daily basis, "How the hell can people do this stuff to animals?"

Shane (what he was later named by a really cute little boy) stayed at the vet hospital for several days until he was mostly recovered and able to come back to the shelter. He was such a sweet, loving cat after recovering from his ordeal. It makes me sick to my stomach when I think about what happened to him. I think about him hunched over, sitting on the side of the road with a broken heart in the pouring rain for hours, waiting for someone to help him. But Shane got what he deserved…a wonderful loving home where he will live out the rest of his life with a kind family.

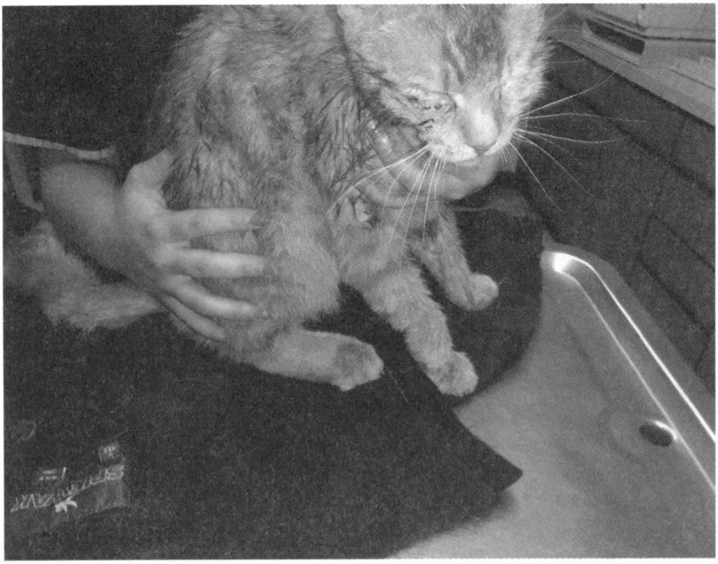

Shane all wet and cold getting checked out at the veterinarian's office, wrapped in my coat.

Shane back at my office purring away, rubbing on his cat carrier with his missing whiskers.

Shane walking around my office loving everyone.

CHAPTER EIGHT

The Love in the Job

Most of the time, my job consists of dealing with people who don't want to see me standing at their front door. People are often rude, uncooperative, and disrespectful. It can be degrading at times to be constantly surrounded by negativity, so when a small positive thing happens, it can go a long way toward restoring my self-worth.

Over a year ago, I responded to a call to check on the welfare of a dog. The caller remained anonymous. The house was a townhome in a low-income neighborhood. I was initially disgusted by the emaciated condition of the dog when I was first welcomed into the house by the owner. The dog was skin and bones. It was an older mixed-breed dog. As I discussed the dog's condition with the owner, it became apparent to me that she wasn't quite "all there." She was very slow and, quite honestly, meant no harm at all; she loved animals and respected them; I could just tell from my years on the job dealing with various people.

When I asked, the lady showed me all the food she had for the dog, and I noticed the dog wasn't interested in eating the food in its bowl. It wasn't acting sick; it was acting as if it just eats as it pleases, and it wasn't hungry. I later found out that the dog had belonged to her recently passed-away mother. It was an ancient dog, sweet as pie, but had to have been pushing fifteen years at least. This sweet lady had a couple of cats of her own, and they all looked healthy, well-fed, and had plenty of toys. I could tell she had purchased the toys from a dollar store or thrift shop and had given the cats used boxes as a play gym. The lady said that she didn't work and was on disability. She didn't drive. She had to take the bus wherever she wanted to go. It just broke my heart to see how honest her heart was and how empty her pocketbook must be.

I couldn't leave the dog in her care—it was in terrible condition. It was so skinny there was pretty much no muscle mass. If its body hadn't already resorted to eating away at organs to stay functioning, it would be soon. The lady actually thanked me for helping him because they wouldn't let her "take him on the bus to go get him help from a veterinarian." I ended up bringing the dog right back to the shelter to be assessed by our vet. I told the lady that I would do just that and keep her updated on my findings.

Now back at the shelter, the veterinarian quickly determined the dog was simply old with cancer, amongst other issues, and unable to absorb the nutrients from its food any longer. The veterinarian recommended humane euthanasia sooner than later, since there was simply no helping the dog any further.

I returned to the owner's house right away to sit down and tell her what the veterinarian suggested. You could tell that she was awfully sad to hear the news, but it took so long for the news to properly register that it just didn't hit home as much as it should have. Right after telling her that the dog should be put to sleep, she scurried off to a different room to get some stuff for him. She came back and handed me several various items, including a half-eaten bag of Pupperoni treats and an old beat-up small bible. She asked me if I could give those to her dog when I put him to sleep. She really wanted me to do it. Typically, I don't take anyone's property at all because it just isn't a good idea, but this was different. She would be so hurt if I didn't take this bible to have by his side when he was put to sleep. She wanted me to keep the bible with his body afterward, so I made her a deal that I would keep it with him but bring it back to her afterward. She was happy with this. After she signed some paperwork, I drove back to the animal shelter.

• • •

I was driving back to the shelter, looking at that old beat-up bible sitting on my dashboard, and shaking my head at how distressed I felt for this poor lady. She had to have been in her later forties with the mentality of a child. I got back to the shelter and went to get the old dog out of its cage. It wagged its tail, happy to see me, but was weak and slow getting around. I, unfortunately, was trained in the euthanasia of animals and had to perform it on quite a regular basis. There were just so many extreme cases for which a gentle passing was the best option. I got a fluffy blanket, had him sit down, and set the bible next to him. He wasn't interested in his Pupperonis, but at least I tried. I first gave him a little shot of tranquilizer to calm him to sleep. He slowly laid down on his blanket as I slid the bible under his head for a pillow. Feeling heartbroken, I injected the euthanasia solution to send him to heaven. My gut hurt more than normal on this one. After a couple minutes of petting him goodbye, I slid the bible back out from under his head, clipped off his collar, and wrapped it around the bible for the poor lady to have.

I returned right back to her apartment, gave her back her bible with his collar, and expressed my condolences. She seemed awfully sad but was relieved because she had recognized he needed help that she couldn't get him. We talked for a little while, and I left her with my business card. Typically, I never give out my work cell phone number to people, but this lady needed to have a direct number to call in the event of a future animal issue. I felt obligated to watch over her to whatever extent I could. So, I hand-wrote my work cell phone on the business card and instructed her to call me if she ever had an emergency with her animals or if she needed a little extra food for them once in a while (We have a food bank for needy people at the shelter). I left it at that.

A month or two went by, and my phone rang with a

number I didn't recognize. I answered the phone and there she was. Wanting to know if her "kitties could have a little food or maybe some litter" because she was almost out. I said sure, and we coordinated a time for me to stop by and drop it off. She would let me in and get so excited I was there, bringing me each one of her cats to greet, and telling me all about her day.

This relationship has been ongoing for close to a year. I heard from her every couple of months for one reason or another. One of the last times she called was when her cat had a hair mat on its back, and she couldn't figure out how to brush it out. I clipped it off for her. The lady was just so heartbreakingly kind and harmless, it brightened my day to know I could help her out every now and again.

The most recent call from her was a week before Christmas on a Friday, but I was tied up with priority calls and couldn't get there until Monday, just a couple of days before Christmas. She needed a little cat litter this time. "That's ok," she always says if it takes a day or two for me to get to her. I pulled up and carried the litter jug to the apartment door and buzzed her apartment for entry into the building. As she welcomed me with excitement, I looked around her apartment at her cute little Christmas tree and old Christmas decorations that I am sure meant so much to her. She brought me "Fluffy" first to say *hi*, and then the other two. Before I left, she ran over to her table and handed me two Christmas cards. One read to the shelter, spelled in an unruly but imaginative way. The other she handed me was for "you." It had my name on the front but was scribbled out, like she couldn't figure out how to spell it and just gave up. *So cute.* I thanked her, feeling so blessed that she had made these cards for the shelter and myself. After I left, I opened the card, which read, "Thank you for helping me," and something about helping the animals in the world, but it was completely spelled wrong and out of phrase, making it unable to be understood. She drew a Christmas tree and what I think was a Santa head in the card. I knew out of any Christmas present I was to receive that year, this would be by far my favorite.

Owner showing me the dog had food and water at her townhome.

Eating canned food at the animal shelter.

CHAPTER NINE

Embedded Collar

A brief warning for this chapter: the end of this chapter contains photographs of the animal I talk about and his injuries which are severe. The photos are graphic, so if you feel that looking at them may cause you anguish, please don't. However, I felt it important to include the images because they are powerful and set a clear example of what will happen if you don't properly care for your pet.

At mid-day, I was dispatched over to a neighborhood in the inner city to pick up a dog with an injury to its neck, according to the caller. I was quite familiar with the neighborhood—not for good reasons. It was a well-known high-crime area. As I got to the house, I was greeted by two younger women who had the pit bull on their front porch. Everyone in the neighborhood was out on their front porches. No one appeared to be at work in this neighborhood. Luckily, it was a friendly dog. He was a blue pit bull mix. I instantly saw the injury was a heavy chain wrapped around and embedded into his neck. I found it sickening. It was by far one of the worst embedded collars I'd seen yet. I was honestly wondering how this dog wasn't dying from some secondary infection. This heavy-duty chain was wrapped around his neck as a collar, and the dog was dragging several feet of chain along with it. Whoever chained him up must not have had a collar, so they just wrapped the chain around his neck as one.

You couldn't help but cringe when you saw how bloody his neck was. The thought of how uncomfortable it must have been dragging that heavy chain that pulled on his gaping wounds around the neck made me nearly sick. I went back to my truck and got my heavy-duty bolt cutters that I use when people padlock their dogs to their chains and such. I proceeded to cut the loose hanging chain off the section that was wrapped around his neck as a collar. Essentially, I had to put my leash around the dog's body because I wouldn't dare pull on this dog's poor neck.

Tenderly, I moved him into my truck before briefly speaking with the two young females who claimed they had found the dog in the nearby park. I suspected they were lying to me, and it was actually their dog, but now wasn't the time for interrogation. I needed to get the dog some immediate medical care. I jotted down the identification of the "finders", trying to be one step ahead in case they were involved.

I brought the dog back to the shelter and was able to

successfully cut off the chain around his neck. All that remained were a couple of links that were too far embedded for me to remove. This poor dog's skin had started to grow around the chain links. The veterinarian had to surgically remove those pieces.

• • •

The next day I went out to complete my investigation and find the responsible party. I planned to target the house where I picked him up first. To do so, I went to all the neighboring houses and questioned residents to ask if they had ever seen the dog before. To my surprise, they all said they hadn't. I then returned to the shelter, made up some reward flyers, and went back to the neighborhood, distributing them door-to-door. Typically, when you offer up money for information, someone is going to say something. I also knew if the dog wasn't from that house, it came from somewhere nearby, because it couldn't have gone far unnoticed dragging that heavy chain and being that severely injured.

Over the next couple of days, I only received tips that didn't pan out from my reward poster distribution. Someone said it was so and so's dog, but when I would go to the house to question the subject, their dog would be standing there beside the owner. I turned to the local media as a last resort. The news aired the reward poster and photos of the dog and requested they contact us with information. It worked. An individual called and said he used to be her dog, but she had to give it away about a year prior when she moved into a rental house that didn't allow the dog. The individual said she gave him to none other than the young woman who called in and claimed she had found the dog.

I returned to the house where I picked him up and was able to talk to my suspect. I began the conversation with, "I know this was your dog, I just want to know why you allowed this to happen."

She instantly started crying and claimed she noticed the collar was bothering his neck, so she began putting peroxide and such on the wound. She said she couldn't afford to take him to the vet, so his condition just got worse and worse until the wound was at its current status. In fear the dog would die, her family member told her to call animal control and lie, saying she found him, so she did. I explained to her I would be pursuing a warrant for her arrest for the animal cruelty to the dog. It took weeks for that dog to begin showing improvement from that injury. The vet techs were constantly tending to his neck with medication.

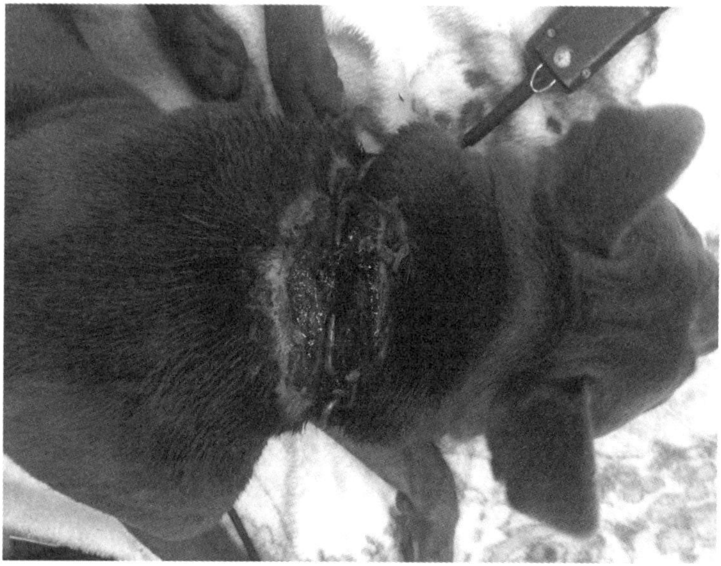

A chain collar was embedded in the dog's neck; upon arrival at the animal shelter, I tranquilized the dog to relieve the pain before cutting the collar off.

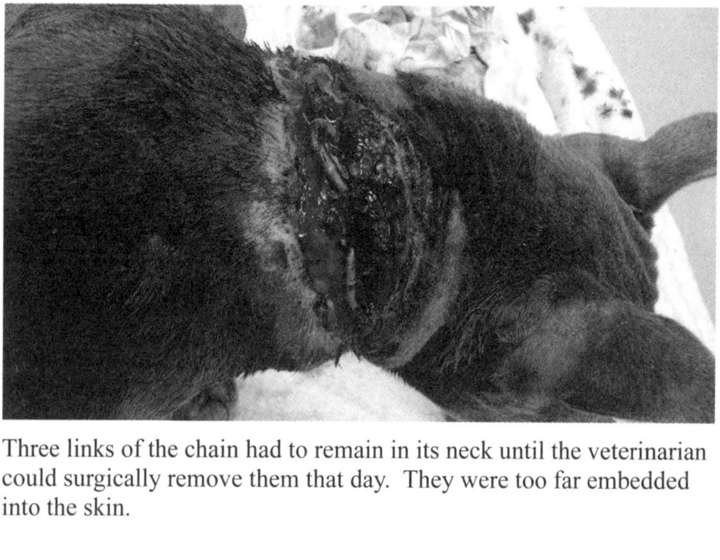

Three links of the chain had to remain in its neck until the veterinarian could surgically remove them that day. They were too far embedded into the skin.

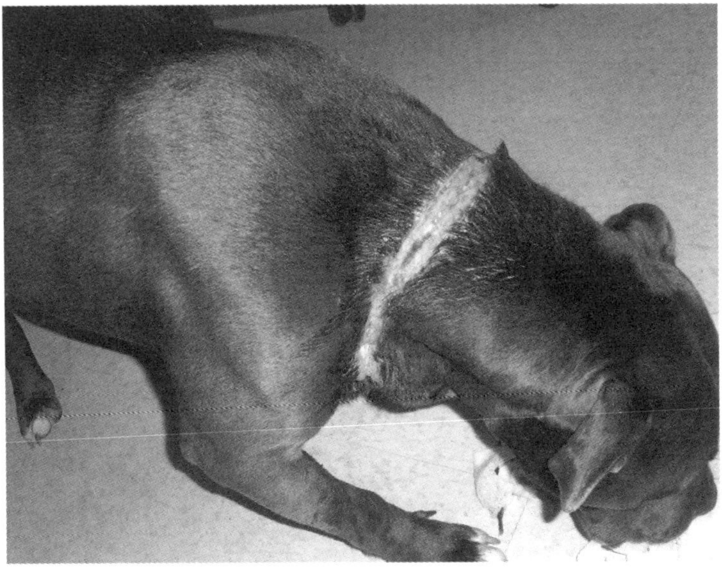

Healing up over a week after treatment!

CHAPTER TEN

Sewer Dog

I was at work one August day, about three in the afternoon. The busy summer was slowing down, but the calls were still trickling in, keeping us busy. I still didn't have time to take an actual lunch break—I'd just eat on the way to the next place. A call came in to dispatch from the city workers saying they had found a dog down in a sewer drain. I was tied up on another investigation, so the dispatcher sent the closest available animal control officer to at least get the dog and get it back to the shelter where it was safe.

The officer arrived on the scene. It was in the north end of the city in a quite unsafe neighborhood. City workers had gathered around this horribly neglected puppy. He was malnourished, weak, covered in mange, missing half of his fur. Scabs covered most of his body. It was heartbreaking to look at the innocent puppy. The city workers explained to the officer that they had heard yipping when they were working in the area. They followed the noise and discovered the puppy inside the sewer. It was one of those round sewer lids with grating that you can see through. The puppy was certainly put in there by someone since there was no other entry point except to remove the lid and drop it in. I've had to remove those sewer lids before to help baby ducks and such—they are heavy, no joke! The officer jotted down all the witnesses' information and put the puppy in his truck to transport it to the shelter for immediate care.

At the shelter, the veterinarian examined the puppy right away. The veterinarian scored the puppy a two out of ten (on a scale of 1 to 10, with ten being the best condition), for his emaciated body condition. This means the puppy was heading towards death due to malnourishment. The puppy had mange, open wounds, and a secondary fungal and bacteria skin infection on top of it.

The case was turned over to me to investigate. We put out a media release with a reward asking for information on an owner or suspects. Tips came in left and right. I spent countless hours responding to the tips that didn't pan out.

• • •

I pulled into the driveway of my next tip. It was another city house, not too far from where the dog was found. A woman who looked to be in her thirties answered the door with attitude from the very start. I explained why I was there and told her that people were alleging she was the owner of the puppy. She turned to her teenage son, laying into him, asking him what the @#%^ was going on, insinuating he knew something. The "classy" mother pretty much threatened her son, saying he'd better tell me what was up or he was going to be in some serious shit with her. Her son proceeded to tell me how this puppy followed him and his friends up to the basketball courts and wouldn't leave them alone. First, one of his friends tied it to the fence while they played basketball. Then, his other friend Tony was bragging to all the guys he was going to put that puppy in the sewer drain. Her son claimed he left with a group of people before it happened, but I was sure there was plenty more he wasn't divulging. He talked me through where Tony lived on such and such street two houses down from the park.

I headed over to Tony's house. As I pulled up, I rolled my eyes to myself and let out a big sigh, like *here we go.* There had to have been at least four or five big dudes drinking "forties" and likely passing blunts sitting on the front porch. I called out to dispatch my location and got out of my truck. I walked up to the guys, made some small talk, and asked if Tony's mom or dad was around. They all said he had a mom, but she wasn't around. I handed over a business card, asking them to have her give me a call about something with Tony. They gave me a nod, saying they'd pass it along.

A day later, I got a call from Tony's mother, who agreed to meet me at the house with Tony. I had told her that Tony was being named in an animal cruelty investigation and I needed to talk to him about it.

Back at the house, Tony and his mother were waiting for me on the porch. He looked scared and she looked pissed at him. I questioned him on his involvement, and he admitted he put the puppy in the sewer as his friend claimed he did. Tony claimed the dog followed him and his friends to the basketball court. He told the dog to leave them alone, but it wouldn't. Tony said his friends told him to tie it to the fence, so he did. His other friend suggested they put it down the drain, so he did. He figured it would die anyway because it looked like it was deathly ill. Three of his friends lifted the heavy sewer drain off and he shoved the puppy down the drain. I had Tony write up a statement and sign it before I left.

As I drove back to the animal shelter that day to type up my report to pursue a felony warrant for his arrest, I just couldn't wrap my head around how a fifteen-year-old boy could take a *puppy* and shove it down a sewer drain to suffer and die. It scares me to think of the pure coldness in that kid's soul (and probable future victims as he becomes an adult). I had to focus on the fact that the puppy was safe now, that I'd be getting the boy arrested for this, it would be on his criminal history, and it would help keep him locked up in years to come when the next arrests come.

CHAPTER ELEVEN

Dog Catchin' for Real

Animal Control often gets calls of dogs running loose in neighborhoods, but typically they wind up being the neighbor's dog that just got out or something of that nature. Rarely in this area, because it's a big city, do we have any "feral" dogs, or dogs that have been on their own so long they resort to natural instincts and a fear of coming anywhere near people.

But for several months straight there was this one dog that just couldn't be caught. It was a Shepard mix-type dog. No one knew where the dog came from, but it was loose in the northern area of the city in a neighborhood prominent with rentals and duplexes—a high turnover of people. We guessed someone may have moved out and left it behind—outside. We realized that it might have gotten away from someone, and they just didn't care enough to look for it. Whatever the reason was, this dog was loose in this area for months. We have all the appropriate equipment and trained officers to capture it, but it was unbelievable how smart and unapproachable this dog was. For months, we couldn't catch it!

Month after month, we would get calls from residents in the area who sighted the dog. We would drive out to try to capture it, but it would never work out. Either the dog would be gone and it would be impossible to find it upon arrival, or the dog would see the truck and bolt off in a "blink and you miss it" kind of way. This was just unheard of, that our department could not capture this dog. In addition to our animal control department, local dog lovers and even a veterinarian or two were trying to capture it as well, but no one could. We exhausted all attempts. We tried using a large group of people which was unsuccessful. We tried feeding it in the same spot every day, but that didn't work. We tried a dog live trap. That didn't work. Nothing worked. We couldn't even get within range to chemically immobilize it with our tranquilizer gun. It was as if the dog knew our animal control trucks from all the times we pursued it. Like a movie where the dog talks and runs away because the "evil" dog catcher is trying to catch it to take it to the pound.

We felt terrible that we could not catch the dog. The reports coming in kept becoming more and more heartbreaking. Sightings of the dog were reported, with many reporting further emaciation. A couple months into it we had a concerned area resident call in to say it had been hit by a car and was now limping in the back end. All we wanted to do more than anything was catch this dog and get it safe, fed, and treated by the veterinarian, but it was unbelievably evasive. For years and years, we had never had such a wild and uncapturable dog.

I went into work one day to my deputy director at the time with a dead serious look on his face, saying, "Suit up and get your tranquilizer gun. We are going to catch this dog. Just me and you in the unmarked white van." I laughed because he was dead serious. He was a stern guy that you didn't want to mess with, retired from years on the police force, now in charge of the animal control officers, but he sure could be funny too. He was like a father figure to me. He knew when not to mess around, but he was a lot of fun at the same time. I remember years ago him sitting in on my job interview along with the director and another person. He intimidated the shit out of me. Anyhow, I proceeded to suit up as instructed. I loaded up a dart with a tranquilizer cocktail inside and racked it into my gun.

There we were, driving down the road, him at the wheel, me in the passenger's seat in my uniform with my tranquilizer gun (which looks similar to a shotgun) secured in between my legs, pointed toward the ceiling. We looked hilarious, like a bunch of idiots in a big ugly white van that smelled like stale dog urine from all the dogs that have peed, pooped, and drooled all over it for a decade or more. As we traveled down the road, heading to the several-block area where the dog had been sighted on a daily basis, he filled me in on the sudden desire to go all out and not go home until the dog was caught. Several people were complaining to local media, commissioners, etc. that we weren't out trying to capture this dog. It had the makings of a political uproar. I was very offended that residents were complaining, but that's politics. We wanted to catch the dog just as much as they wanted it caught. So far, we had devoted countless hours, resources, and staff to the goal of capturing this dog. How insulting they were pretty much saying we weren't doing anything about it when we were doing just the exact opposite. My director really wanted it caught because she was getting a lot of heat from the commissioners.

• • •

Now in the area, we began patrolling for the dog. We were laughing and joking the entire time because you can only imagine the looks we got from people when we were rolling through a neighborhood in a big ugly white van at ten miles an hour, staring around as if stalking the area. This went on for quite a while with absolutely no sighting of the dog. My deputy director commented in a disappointed voice, "Damnit, this was a big waste of time," sounding as if losing hope quickly. Circling through the area over and over, looking everywhere for the dog, we would reach the main busy one-way road and then pull out, go up a block, and begin the circle again. We were losing hope with every patrol through the few blocks of the area. Giving it one more chance, we pulled onto the busy one-way, remaining in the side lane of four so we could turn back into the neighborhood that we pulled out of. Just as we pulled out onto the busy road, my deputy director yelled, "Holy shit, there's the dog!"

It was like we saw the president standing in a parking lot. There was excitement and a few swear words, followed by a calming pep talk ("game time"). Not to put the pressure on, the boss hollers to me, "Do not miss." I click off the safety on my tranquilizer gun while rolling down my window, and then getting my upper half out of the window, aiming with my gun toward the dog as my boss pulled into the parking lot and slowly rolled up within range. The dog hadn't noticed us since it was such a busy area with cars whizzing by. The dog was simply wandering. There was no trying to catch the dog, trying to sweet talk it into the vehicle, or trying to approach it—we had done that over and over. We had to get a tranquilizer dart into it—it was the only way, and we knew that. It was the humane thing to do at this point. The dog needed to be caught, and it needed vet care—it needed to be rescued.

Partially out the window with the dog in my sight, I watched as the dog crept up slowly, just feet away from being in range. The dog hadn't noticed us yet, but that could change at any time. I would have just seconds to take the shot if it noticed us and tried to bolt off. I was ready. Now just in range, the dog started to show signs of becoming alert. I took the shot. With a perfect shot, my dart stuck right in the muscle mass on the back leg where it would simply be an ouch-prick for a couple of seconds to the dog. The dog took off immediately upon the dart making contact. Not only did it take off, but it took off in the opposite direction of the busy four-lane one-way road we needed to access to follow it.

"Shit," I thought. Within seconds I threw my gun nearly on my deputy director and bailed out of the van, running faster than I ever have. There was no way, absolutely no way, I was going to let this dog get away. It wasn't an easy run with all my gear on—a belt with my radio, baton, and all my tools of the trade, plus my combat boots, bulletproof vest, and long pants. It was not easy, but I ran. I knew that with the dog's adrenalin up, it could be a couple of minutes before this dog started slowing down and becoming affected by the drugs. I kept my eye on the dog, running through apartment complexes and parking lots. The dog even jumped a chain-link fence that got in my way. I was paying no attention to anyone watching and laughing. I could just hear some guy saying, "Holy shit, those dog catchers in this county don't mess around."

Several blocks later and completely out of breath, I could see the dog up ahead slowing down and starting to stagger. I couldn't believe it! I knew I had it. I couldn't wait to call my deputy director up, who was likely driving around with no idea where the dog and I were since he didn't have a radio in the van. He was going to be ecstatic. For months we were trying to catch this poor dog. I slowed my pursuit as the dog slowed to a staggering walk. I wanted to leave it alone until it fell asleep completely. Until it fell asleep completely, I couldn't be sure that if I startled it, adrenalin would counteract the drugs, and it might take off again. A minute later, it finally laid down. I pulled out my phone and called my deputy director, still completely out of breath, "We got it!"

He drove the few blocks over to where we were, and we lifted the sleeping dog into the back of the van. Meanwhile, *ugh*, a lady who happened to be in the parking lot of the weed (marijuana) store where, apparently, we originally shot it with the tranquilizer dart, had witnessed the whole thing. She was screaming and crying that we just, "Pulled up and shot that dog! (We) were so cruel," she said.

It took me several minutes to explain the story to the lady. I felt terrible that she thought we were some mean dog catchers just out shooting at a dog that was minding its own business in a parking lot. After she realized what the entire story was, I think she somewhat got it, but you could tell she still had a chip on her shoulder, not understanding completely.

Off we drove, ecstatic to be getting this dog some help. As we loaded it into the van, completely knocked out asleep, we realized we hadn't brought a thing to confine it in. No kennel, no chain, pretty much if the drugs wore off, we were screwed. We had a good laugh at ourselves for that. Both of us are planners who don't make stupid mistakes like that. We drove it right to a local vet before the drugs wore off, which worked out well because we were going to get it checked out anyway. They took some quick x-rays and treated the dog for some minor concerns. All in all, the dog was in exceptional shape for living on its own for such a long time. This dog was a true fighter. It stayed at the vet's office for the night. I had my deputy director snap a quick photo of me and the dog in its cage at the vet since its drugs were wearing off.

On our way back to the shelter, we were feeling pretty damn proud of ourselves; I'm not going to lie. Not that we did anything exceptional—we just finally were in the right place at the right time, finally with an opportunity to tranquilize it. We decided to call the director to inform her of the excellent news. We knew she'd be so relieved. We joked, "Good news, we got the dog, and it's at the vet. Bad news, we may be on YouTube tonight looking like brutal dog hunters," we told her.

Within a couple of days, the director had found the dog an excellent loving home with a *securely* fenced yard. The adopters were educated dog trainers and were so excited to work with the dog and tame it back into a loving pet. Case closed.

CHAPTER TWELVE

The Cold, Dark Basement

I returned a phone call to a cable installer who called our dispatch line wanting to report cruelty he had just witnessed on his job. I began talking to the man who said he was called to a rental house in not the greatest part of the city for a cable installation job that day. In order to run the cable through the house, he had to go into the basement. The cable installer said he began heading down to the basement, as is routine in the job. He flicked on the light and made his way down the stairs into the dreary, cold basement. As he reached the last few steps, he stopped dead in his tracks, horrified by what he had stumbled across. He saw two pit bulls that he described to me as, "The skinniest dogs I have ever seen." He knew something wasn't right with the dogs the way they cowered at his presence. He said there was an open bag of dog food off to the side and he couldn't help but sneak them both a handful of since one was tied up and the other in a wire crate. The cable installer quickly pulled out his cell phone and snapped pictures of the dogs to send me. I was so impressed by what he had done. I knew time was of the essence in this case since he had just witnessed this a few hours prior. If it would result in a needed search warrant, I would have to obtain it as quickly as possible to convince the judge that the evidence was fresh, and it was very likely the dogs were still in the basement. I needed to get there as soon as possible.

Typically, I respond to complaints and investigate them by myself, but for this one, I had my partner meet me around the corner from the house for a few different reasons. Some people are simply more compliant when more than one uniform is at their front door, and if they weren't going to be compliant, I knew I would need someone to watch the house while I left to get a search warrant. If I didn't have someone to watch the house, they could easily just remove the dogs when I left. In addition, this was not a good neighborhood. I suspected the individuals I would be dealing with would be the opposite of happy to see a law enforcement uniform at their door—especially one likely to seize their dogs.

I called out my badge number and reported to my dispatcher over the radio that I had arrived at the address. I walked up to the front door and knocked. A younger male who had to be in his early twenties answered the door. He certainly was no upstanding citizen. He gave me attitude from the minute he opened the door, acting "hood." I told him that I'd received a complaint about the welfare of the dogs in the basement, and that I needed to take a look at them.

He responded, "There ain't no dogs here."

I thought to myself, *Oh, here we go.* I took a step back, tilted my head dramatically, looked at the house numbers on the house and read them out loud. Then I replied, trying not to be a smart ass like he was being, but with confidence, "Yes, there are two dogs in your basement, and I need to take a look at them."

He continued with his, "I don't know what you're talkin' 'bout; there ain't no dogs here." This went on for several minutes until I ended the conversation.

I put on a serious face, and in a confident tone, I told him, "I know there are two dogs in the basement here, and we are not walking away from this until we look at those two dogs."

The guy got an "Oh shit" look on his face and started backpedaling, realizing his lie was not going to work. Now he claimed, "Umm, I don't live here, and I don't know nothing about no dogs here. I am only watching the kids here."

I looked at him with an even more serious face and said, "Here's what I am going to do. My partner and I are going to go sit out in our trucks, me on this side of the house and him on the other side. We will continue to sit outside of the house for no more than fifteen minutes. If no one wants to come talk to me and claim ownership of the dogs in the basement and let me see them by the time fifteen minutes is up, I will be leaving while yet another officer takes my place. I will go request a search warrant from the judge, ordering you to let me in to take a look." Both my partner and I turned around and walked away and proceeded as I had explained.

I called my partner, who was sitting just on the other side of the house. We may or may not have made bets on how long it would take for someone to come out and commented to each other in a derogatory voice, "Man, there ain't no dogs in this house." I watched the blinds in the house crack open every few minutes as if people were looking out to see if we were serious.

After ten minutes went by, I began losing hope that my plan of them complying was going to work. I called in for another officer to start heading in my direction to take my place while I went to start typing up a search warrant. Just shy of fifteen minutes later, an old beat-up truck flew up to the house and rip-roared into the driveway. I watched as two younger males got out of the truck and began walking toward mine. "Game time," I radioed to my partner. These guys were even worse to deal with than the first one.

The one guy immediately approached me, saying, "What's the problem?!" I asked him if the dogs in the basement belonged to him, and he said, "Yeah, and they are fine; why?"

I told him that I needed to see them and verify that they were, in fact, "fine." He continued to question me, saying they were fine and I didn't need to see them, but I was persistent and finally won. To my surprise, he actually let me into the house and led me to the basement to see the dogs.

As my partner and I walked through the front door, the typical smell of a drug house was prevalent. The stale odor of marijuana and air freshener recently sprayed was in the air. People who were frequenting the house were sitting around on the one couch and a few folding chairs, looking nervous as we walked in, waiting for their opportunity to dart out the door. One girl I laid eyes on was disappointing. It was a girl who I had previously met when she was locked up in a juvenile facility where I had once worked. I had much higher hopes for her than this. She looked at me, but I didn't say anything, just lightly nodded my head so as not to call her out in front of her people, but at the same time saying hello to her because I care. I could see in her face that she was embarrassed and wanted to say "hi" but couldn't because it would be frowned upon by her companions.

I was first down the basement stairs with the owner leading the way, my partner not far behind. In the first open area of the basement was the first dog. It was a pit bull tied with a heavy tow chain to a metal support post. The tow chain couldn't have been more than two or three feet long. He could hardly move. The dog was excited to see us, but hesitant at the same time. The dog raised itself off the cement floor where he lay with nothing but the cold floor beneath him, wagging his tail and holding up his back leg, obviously very injured. He didn't have any food or water and could barely stand up due to the short, heavy chain. As I got closer to the dog, I noticed scars and bite wounds, primarily covering his face and front legs. I realized at that point what these dogs were being used for. They weren't pets—they were likely his fighting dogs.

I continued on to the next room, where the other dog was confined in a small dog crate. There was no bottom in the kennel, just feces and urine that she was lying directly in. Both dogs were thin, not the worst that I've seen, but inexcusably underweight. This other dog was also scarred from fighting. Her one eye was red and infected. This dog was also lacking any food or water.

Before I said anything, the owner started commenting that they got into it with each other the other day, and that is why they were like they were—a common excuse of a dogfighter. It was just common for an abuser to make excuses for their conditions before I could even say anything. I am no dummy, though; the scars, old and new, tell a different story—that they had been fought more than one time. My partner and I didn't have to say a word to each other. We knew we would be seizing these dogs for multiple violations.

We pulled out our dog leashes, explaining to the owner that the dogs were being seized for the lack of veterinary care, the lack of dog licenses, the improper tethering, the neglect of not providing adequate food, the unsanitary conditions the one was confined in, and so on. As we began walking the dogs up the steps, trying to make a quick, safe exit from the house, the owner and his friend began running their mouths, saying that we were only taking their dogs because we were targeting them and so on. I wanted to respond and put him in his place for the stupid comments, but I knew that would only escalate the situation. I knew deep down *he knew* that he screwed up but just had to put on a scene to look cool in front of his friends. I told him that he could express that concern when this got to the courtroom.

Back at the shelter, the dogs thrived with adequate food, but unfortunately, the prognosis wasn't good. One had a broken leg that was healing incorrectly. The poor thing sat in that basement for who knows how long with that broken leg. Both had become extremely aggressive (Extreme Dog Aggression is a thing in my world), and were deemed unsafe to adopt out.

CHAPTER THIRTEEN

Sheltie

The staff came into the shelter first thing in the morning and found a pitiful little Sheltie dog tied up to a signpost just outside the front door of the animal shelter. It's not extremely uncommon for this to occur, but it's always just as sad each time. The dog was nervous and a little scared but so very sweet, just polite. She was dragging her back paw and barely using the leg, obviously injured. Figuring the dog was abandoned by its owner due to the injury, the staff brought her in and got her into a cozy bed until our veterinarian could look at her.

A bit later, my boss asked me to drive the dog to a local veterinarian for x-rays since we didn't have an x-ray machine at the shelter at the time. Without an x-ray machine, our shelter veterinarian couldn't clearly diagnose her injury. She was such a timid sweet dog that I didn't have the heart to put her in the back part of the animal control truck, where it is likely pretty dark and scary. She rode right up in the front seat, oddly, as if she had done it a million times. She sat quietly, watching out the window as if riding in the front seat and going for car rides was a regular occurrence for her. We chit-chatted on the way about how cute she was. I probably looked like a lunatic at stoplights, but I didn't care. We arrived at the vet's office and I gave the dog a little hug. I dropped her off to get her x-rays and probably stay for the night.

The next day, I went to work in the early morning. It was only my dispatcher and myself in the building as I proceeded into my office to prepare for my shift. As I took my shotgun out of the safe and grabbed my clipboard filled with all the places I needed to go that day, I heard the shelter veterinarian come through the front door and pass through the hallway heading back to her surgery suite. As I gathered my things a short while later and walked out of my office, I glanced up and saw an elderly man sitting in the dimly lit front lobby, as if waiting patiently to be helped. I was confused and caught off guard because we were obviously closed, and no one was around. I quickly realized the veterinarian must not have securely shut the front door when she came in, allowing this man access.

I walked up to the front lobby and asked him if I could help him. This man was so sweet. He asked me, "Is Paris okay?" I had no idea what he was talking about until he continued, saying in a slow manner, "I brought Paris here so you guys could help her because her leg got hurt."

Pointing to the sign in front, he said, "I tied her on that sign and put her favorite bone out there with her." With my guard up at first, a little mad that he would just tie her up in front of a shelter, my outlook quickly changed when I realized how very innocent he was, simply trying to get his beloved dog help from the shelter where he believed they help dogs. This man was so sweet and pitiful. Over the years, I have learned to pick out a bullshitter over a genuinely caring person quickly, and this man was purely innocent—one of the kindest people I had run across in a while.

He went on to tell me all about Paris, that "She is my dog," and she liked to have her teeth brushed with chicken toothpaste every night before bed. He went on to tell me her favorite snack was ice cream cones from McDonald's. "We get a lot of ice cream," he said, as a grin came across his face. This man nearly brought tears to my eyes. Everything in me had to choke back the tears that wanted to just stream down my face due to his pure innocence and clear love for his dog. We continued to converse for quite a while, until he seemed to finally get enough courage to say what he seemed to be dreading to ask: "Did you have to put her down?" A terribly sad look came across his face, as he seemed to be preparing himself for some dreadful news about his true best friend.

When I told him she was just fine so far, you couldn't have wiped the grin off his face. He told me the story about what happened to her that night. "We were sitting on the porch listening to the baseball game on the boombox radio like we do. She was in her chair next to me and when she jumped off her chair, she hurt her leg. I thought if we just went to bed, she would be okay in the morning, but I woke up around midnight and she was still really hurt, so I brought her here so you guys could fix her."

After getting his contact information, I assured him I'd be reaching out when I could and sent him on his way.

A day or so later after the x-rays came back, showing a typical muscle injury that needed nothing more than some daily medications and rest—no jumping off tall things—we called the man to have him come pick her up. We prepared enough medication and labeled how he should give it daily until we could have him come in to do a follow up exam. I told him I would have to stop by every couple of days and check on her to make sure everything was going okay (just to be a hundred percent sure she was in good hands). You could hear the joy in his voice when I told him to come pick her up. He told me he was at the laundry mat, but he was just going to put his wet laundry in the car and come. The last thing he cared about was drying his laundry. I reminded him not to let her jump up onto anything, so she couldn't damage her leg any further.

A few days later I stopped by his house and knocked, but he didn't seem to be around. The house was nothing extravagant at all, but it was obviously well looked after, as if he took pride in the little he had. It was an older trailer in the trailer park. As I was knocking on the door, I was glancing around as all law enforcement does, taking in the scene and analyzing. What caught my eye was four pieces of freshly sawed-off wood. *It couldn't be,* I thought to myself. I left him a typical notice on the door, saying I had stopped by and to call me with a better time to return. It wasn't ten minutes after I had left that I got a call from him saying, "We are home and can you come back and see us," sounding so excited. I turned around and arrived back a few minutes later.

He greeted me at the door and invited me in. There was Paris, so happy in her loving home. Just as I suspected earlier from my observations—there sat his recliner, and right next to his chair sat hers. I wanted to cry it was so cute. The chair seat (a normal human chair) was literally a couple inches from the floor. He had sawed the legs off of it so she didn't have to jump up on her chair and hurt her leg. What an absolute sweet ending to this story. Those two were two peas in a pod.

CHAPTER FOURTEEN

Grizzly Cuddle Bear

I was traveling to the north end of the city for a loose stray dog complaint. These are generally boring calls. For example, someone sees a dog running down the street and calls to report seeing it. I would say about ninety percent of the time, we never find the dog. By the time we get the call, it gets dispatched out to one of us, and when we get to the area, the dog is always long gone. Most of the time we are so backed up on calls that it could be a day or two before we even have an officer able to respond to the call. That probably sounds crazy, although it's the case, but there are typically only one or two of us at any time responding to calls, covering the entire county—with me primarily only assigned to handle the cruelty or neglect calls.

Calls must be prioritized and responded to in the order

they are received and the emergence of the situation. If we have someone calling in that they were attacked by a dog, or maybe the police are raiding a house and need our assistance, we have to go to those calls before we can go drive around looking for a dog that is frolicking around a neighborhood. The priority calls are so often coming in one right after the other that these patrols are often not responded to until a day or two later.

• • •

I rounded the corner onto the street where this dog was reported to have been running loose a couple of days prior. The caller reported the dog to be “a big black dog running loose in the 400 block” of the street. As I pulled down the street and began patrolling for the big black dog, a light bulb clicked on in my head. I recognized the very short couple-block street. When you respond to calls all day, every day for years, you begin to remember who lives where and what dogs they have from previous dealings. In this case, that is exactly what happened. As I drove down this two-block road, one house stuck out to me. I remembered responding to a welfare concern at that house a year or two prior, but the rest was fuzzy.

I pulled over on the side of the road near the house and ran a history check on the address in my computer. Sure enough, we had dealt with the residents about a year prior, and they had a black Newfoundland named Grizzly at that time, “a big black dog.” I had written the owner a citation for not having a dog license and did some education on the proper housing and care of the dog. I remembered

Grizzly being thinner than he should have been, but not thin enough to actually take enforcement action.

I decided I was going to stop and be nosy because it was likely Grizzly running loose, and I wanted to take advantage of the opportunity to check up on him and see how he was doing. When I pulled into the driveway, the house was to my right, and directly ahead, sitting back at the end of the driveway was an old garage with shed doors. The doors were open, and there stood Grizzly, just a couple of steps outside the garage. He was on a chain tied up in the garage, but he could reach a few feet outside. There were no cars in the driveway, and there didn't seem to be anyone home.

I got out of my truck and went to the door to knock. Grizzly was very protective, barking and growling at this stranger in a big scary uniform walking in his yard. He was doing a good job of protecting me because even I was a little on edge, hoping he wouldn't break free from his chain because he was a large dog who really didn't want me in his yard. I knocked several times on the house door, but no one answered. As I stood at the door waiting for an answer, I didn't like what I was seeing from a distance. I went back to my truck to grab some dog treats. I was going to try to win Grizzly over so I could check on him. It was bitterly cold outside, and I had to make sure he had a doghouse or somewhere to get to for shelter/warmth. An open, uninsulated garage with a dirt floor was not sufficient shelter. Furthermore, I noticed Grizzly's facial features seemed more sunken than they should. I could make out his body shape from the distance away, and it was concerning. Newfoundlands, which Grizzly was, have very thick, long hair, which should make it near impossible to see their body shape (if they are skinny or not).

I began approaching Grizzly in a calm quiet way, telling him I was alright, not here to cause him any trouble. The sweet talking and calm approach didn't seem to make much of an impact. He continued to bark and threaten with his body language, warning me not to come near him. I pulled out my bag of squishy, stinky dog treats, and slowly tossed one over to him. He gobbled it up before I could blink. *Excellent,* I thought to myself, *I can win him over with treats.* I slowly crept closer to his area, tossing him a treat every couple steps.

Within a minute, his behavior had noticeably changed to, "Hmm, maybe this person isn't so bad." Grizzly had stopped barking and threatening me as I continued to approach him, stopping just a couple of inches beyond the reach of his chain. He was still watching me and not fully trusting me, but he was very interested in the treats I continued to win him over with. Within another minute, Grizzly was eating one out of my hand, then another, then another, and then a slight tail wag. Grizzly was starting to realize I was a *good* stranger. I was able to pet Grizzly for a second on his head and reward him with a treat. Within another minute, Grizzly and I were best of friends. His attitude had changed from "I will mess you up if you come on my property" to "I love you" in five minutes. Winning dogs over is just something you have to learn over the years. After years of dealing with them, it just starts to come naturally.

I glanced into the garage where his chain was attached. Old junk/trash all over and a dirt floor, absolutely nothing for him to keep warm in, and a bone-dry water bowl laid near him. I was not impressed. As I glanced in his area, I slowly petted him, running my hand down his back. Doing so, was absolutely shocked. He was nothing but skin and bones underneath that thick long coat. My original observation of his face was that it was sunken from his muscles wasting away. My heart sank for this poor dog. He was going for a ride out of here and never coming back.

Grizzly gladly left his chain and family in the dust. I taped a notice on the owner's door saying the dog had been impounded and to contact me. Grizzly and I got back to the shelter and walked on the scale when we arrived. He weighed sixty-six pounds. This is about half of what this large breed dog should weigh. This would be similar to a one-hundred-and-fifty-pound human weighing seventy pounds. It got better. As I was taking photos of him and doing the typical impound requirements, Grizzly yipped in pain when I stroked his head and ran my hand over his ear. The kennel assistant and I carefully lifted his ear and found green puss coming out of his ears. His ears were so infected that the smell could make an average person vomit. Grizzly's heartworm test showed strongly positive for heartworms. He was a mess on so many levels.

While I continued the intake of his requirements,

I brought him a bowl of water, remembering he didn't have any at his house. Grizzly slopped up the entire bowl of water without taking a breath. He looked up at me, begging for more with his sad eyes. He devoured his food just as fast, of course.

Throughout the next five days at the shelter, Grizzly gained over ten pounds because he was simply being fed an adequate amount of food and given water. Even with the ten pounds added on, he was still extremely underweight. Every day, he filled out more and more, eventually getting to an acceptable weight for his breed. He was treated for heartworms and turned out to be a magnificent dog.

The owner was charged with animal neglect after I typed up my report and secured a warrant.

Grizzly was adopted by the nicest family ever, and I so appreciated the follow-up photos they would send. The last photo was of him grilling hot dogs with his owners at their beautiful log home. He has the life he has always deserved now.

CHAPTER FIFTEEN

More Cows

There are very few times that I cry about what I see on this job. Over the years, you just see so much; your mind somehow gets used to seeing the suffering, pain, and helplessness of animals. The horrible things I see motivate me to push harder and do thorough investigations so nothing is refutable in court, and there's a strong chance the person will be restricted from owning animals. As a matter of fact, it has been years since I have had to go to court for a full-blown jury trial. I do such thorough investigations that the defendant's attorney tells them it's not even worth it to try to argue in court. The prosecutor's office does a great job negotiating as well. In this case, though, I will admit, I cried on my way home that day.

I received a call out in the country to check on the welfare of some cows. The call came in through an anonymous letter in the mail saying the cows all looked very hungry and skinny. Driving out to the farm, I figured they were probably just dairy cows that some people don't realize look thin. You are supposed to see hip bones and a few ribs in dairy cows—it's their body build. Now, I should admit, I am no cow expert. I know the basics when it comes to cows, but I always turn to an expert when I have a serious concern. This day's visit resulted in just that—a serious concern.

Prior to responding to a house on a complaint, I routinely run the address to see if we have been there before. If we had, I study why, and what happened. This house did show we had been there before. It was a year prior, and it was for a similar concern. The officer who responded to it resolved the complaint by educating and warning the individual on proper care of the cows. They were thin last year, but the officer closed out the complaint after he required the owner to increase hay consumption on the cows and followed up weeks later to see improvement. With that background, being called back was not a good sign.

Coming up to the house, I pulled into the driveway and put my truck in park. I instantly started scanning and observing, as you learn to do in law enforcement. To my left were several calf huts with cattle panels wrapped around to make small enclosures for calves. My first observation was a dead calf lying in one of the pens. And then another. There were a couple of live calves, but they didn't look healthy. I immediately grew concerned and radioed for my boss to start heading out. She was an expert when it came to cows, and I had a feeling I was walking into something bad. I couldn't see the actual cow herd yet. They seemed to be in the barnyard behind the large barn which was blocking my view.

I approached the farmhouse and knocked on the door. An elderly man came to the door, claiming the cows all belonged to his adult son, who lived up the road at a different house. The elderly man could hardly get around, so I didn't press him much on this situation. I drove down the road to where the old man said the owner lived and told him I needed him to come down to the farm. He was compliant—came right down and started showing me around as I asked him to do. He didn't have much of an excuse for the dead calves. He and I began walking towards the barnyard as my boss showed up.

We walked around the barn to discover some of the most disgustingly emaciated cows I have ever seen. I didn't even have words to say to the owner for a while. There was no excuse. The cows were licking their empty troughs, licking each other, sifting through manure, trying to pull out tiny scraps of already digested and shit-out hay. It was deplorable. I instructed the cow owner to start feeding the cows immediately. He did. He knew he was in big trouble and didn't even bother trying to talk his way out of any of it. There were dead cows and cows that appeared down and unable to get up. I knew I was removing these cows from the property and knew I would be arguing in court that this suspect is not to own cows anymore.

While we were on the property, one particular cow was clearly so ill it was miserable. I made the owner call his veterinarian immediately. I later found out his veterinarian hadn't been to the farm for years and was only out then to do some minor breeding-type care. The veterinarian told the owner over the phone that, from what he was describing, the cow needed to be put down immediately. The veterinarian gave him the option of shooting the cow (which, if done correctly, causes immediate death) or having him come out and euthanize it. The veterinarian was tied up on other work and wouldn't be able to come out for a while. The owner had to shoot it. My boss and I stood by and watched this poor cow get blown out of its misery. I had never seen a cow shot and killed before, and hoped I never would again. It took everything I had not to cry watching that poor cow hanging its head, so ill it couldn't walk. It was struggling to even stay standing. Watching it instantly fall to its death as it was shot is something that will forever be engrained in my head.

I had a suspicion there were a lot more dead cows somewhere on the property. I just knew it. He couldn't have possibly had this many cows in such rough shape and not have a pile of dead ones around somewhere. I asked him where he buried his cows, and he pointed out to the field several acres back. I told him to show me, and he looked nervous. We walked back to discover numerous dead cows. Some recently dead, others that had been there for a while. I interrogated the owner about each cow individually, asking what had caused the death, and I was mortified by his responses. One cow had given birth, and her uterus had come out with the calf. The owner said the cow was unable to get up, and the uterus had frozen to the ground in the cold weather. He said he put a chain around her neck and drug her back so he could shoot her outside of the barnyard area. Later he admitted she was alive when he wrapped the chain around her neck, but she was dead by the time he dragged her several acres back. *What person could do that, drag a cow by its neck until it choked to death?* I was beyond disgusted with this guy but kept my composure as I was required to. Another one or two cows had a round bale fall on their heads and crush them. He placed the round bale in a square feeder, so as the cows ate the bottom away, the main part of the bale had fallen on a couple of their heads and likely crushed them or suffocated them to death. I had heard enough. I coordinated for removal of all the cows from the property.

That night on my way home from work, I was covered in cow manure and sweat from all the work that came with this call. Driving down the road, I couldn't choke back the tears in my eyes when I thought of that cow being dragged to its death and the horrible things the rest had endured in his care.

I had necropsies (animal autopsies) done on a few of the dead calves and found they had starved to death. The owner was charged with animal cruelty and ordered by the judge not to own any cows for years. I always think about the terrible things that happened to the other cows on that property before I got involved, and it makes me sick. But I also wonder how many cows I saved from further suffering, and that is a win.

CHAPTER SIXTEEN

Oscar the Weiner Dog

Some of the most difficult cases to prosecute are those of animal abuse. Animal abuse is hitting, beating, or otherwise being cruel to an animal. Neglect, on the other hand, is obvious. The animals that are skin-and-bones or the animals that have obvious untreated medical issues are another thing. But with abuse, how do you prove in court that someone is beating their dog without any physical evidence? Or, typically, how do you prove abuse when we just have one witness who calls in anonymously to report it? Once in a while, you will find a dog with injuries, or even a bruise, as a result of the hitting, but this isn't very common. Despite these things, animals are just so resilient to abuse it's amazing.

In order to remove someone's animal from their home due to abuse, you must be able to prove it in court. You have to have either physical evidence of this, such as veterinary documentation of the injury to the dog indicating abuse, or you have to have some damn good witnesses that saw it happen and will come to court to testify to that. Another option is getting a confession from the suspect. Sometimes even having one witness to say that it happened isn't enough. It would be the owner's word against the witness, who is often a relative or ex-girlfriend, that the defense attorney argues is lying to retaliate.

This day, the call was different. The first call came in to my dispatcher, "My drunken neighbor just beat his dog." Then a second call, "I was driving by this house and saw a man abusing his dog." Excellent I thought to myself, two witnesses who are unrelated. Two witnesses that have no idea the other is calling. Fantastic. It's not a neighbor's word against a dog owner. It's a neighbor's word plus a second witness, a random passerby who has no idea the neighbor called or who this man is in the first place. No arguing the neighbor was just mad and trying to get back at another neighbor or anything. This was looking like a solid animal abuse case.

I promptly responded to the house. When I first arrived at the scene, I went to the neighbor's residence that had called and spoke to them about what they saw. The woman told me she was sitting on her front porch and began hearing yelling and then a dog yelping. She told me she couldn't even believe what she saw. Her neighbor, about three houses down, who was known to always be intoxicated—the neighborhood drunk—stormed out onto his front porch with his wiener dog in hand. He was yelling at it and proceeded to punch it over and over before throwing it off the porch in a rage.

The second caller who I talked to on the phone had the same story. She wasn't from the area, nor did she have any idea someone else reported/witnessed the incident. I knew from these two witness statements this incident surely happened, and it wasn't just some neighborhood dispute or one person dramatizing a story in an attempt to get someone's dog taken away.

I called for another officer to back me up as I proceeded to the suspect's residence. I was quite sure I would be removing the dog from the home and expected I would be dealing with an intoxicated, belligerent man who could become enraged with me for removing his dog.

Once my fellow officer arrived, we walked up the steps and onto the front porch. The door was wide open, with only the screen door shut. The little wiener dog (Dachshund), who was now inside, ran up to the screen door, barking and crying out at our presence. It didn't seem to be limping or showing any indications of being obviously injured, but again, dogs can mask their pain quite well.

I observed a man lying on the couch, fitting the description of what the witness told me, appearing to be "passed out" drunk, wearing only a pair of shorts. I looked at my partner behind me and said, "Well, this is going to be interesting."

We knocked over and over, and the man finally came to. Getting up looking dazed and confused, he scuffled to the door. We proceeded to identify ourselves, and explained to him why we were at his house today. We told him we had a couple of calls from concerned individuals who saw the incident that took place a short while ago with the dog. I was talking in a slow, simple manner so he could follow what I was saying, without allowing him to get a word in.

The man tried to slur a bunch of nonsense, but I asked him what had occurred that prompted him to punch his dog and throw it off the porch in a rage. He fumbled around in a drunken stupor and said the dog shit on the floor in the house. While conversing, I told him we needed to see and check on the dog. The drunk allowed his dog outside after fastening a leash. My partner took the leash and began inspecting the dog.

After talking with the owner for a short while, I went into my closing speech: that the dog would be coming with us today, he was being seized as evidence, needed to be checked out by a veterinarian, and that we would contact him further on likely court proceedings. I kept my even-keeled attitude, never being rude, but maintaining control of the conversation. I knew it really didn't matter how hard I tried with this guy. There wasn't any reasoning with a hammered dude.

My partner handed me the dog leash, and I began heading to the truck to secure the dog in it. My partner remained midway between me and the porch as I walked away, creating somewhat of a barrier with his body language so the suspect wouldn't follow or try to do anything stupid. My partner's positioning was standard procedure.

As I was walking to the truck and opening a side compartment to secure the dog in, the man began to make a scene in a drunken stupor. He was screaming, "You can take that wiener and shove it up your ***," and, "It's not like I cooked him on the grill." He continued, "I don't even care! If you think I am going to pay any money to get that dog back, I don't even want it." This went on until we drove away and, who knows, maybe after. Just another day's work. I've got to give the guy credit; he came up with some pretty witty comments for as drunk as he was.

That dog was the cutest little goofy dog back at the shelter. He was loved by everyone and got adopted right away. Typical little Dachshund!

CHAPTER SEVENTEEN

Fleas, Fleas, and More Fleas

Dispatch radioed me to respond to a general welfare complaint. Whoever called wanted me to check on a few dogs said to be in the house of concern. The house was in the middle of the city on a typical street with houses right next to each other. The complainant (the person who called) wanted to remain anonymous and mentioned concerns about not seeing anyone come to the house in almost a week. They were concerned about the dogs in the house not being cared for.

Prior to my arrival, I pulled over on the side of the road, leaned over, and punched in the address in my truck computer. I wanted to see if we'd been there for prior calls. We had, in fact, been there one time about a year prior, and it had been for a welfare check then, too. The officer who responded to that complaint educated the owner on how to provide proper care for the dogs. There was mention of fleas and inadequate shelter since the dogs were being housed outside at that time. The owner had told the officer she was laid off from her job, amongst other excuses, and was barely getting by with the dogs. The welfare issues with the dogs were not strong enough to remove the dogs from the home or press criminal charges on that day a year ago. The officer, therefore, educated the owner and made sure she obtained dog houses, flea preventative, and dog licenses through our low-cost programs.

I also checked the licensing system prior to arrival and found two expired dog licenses had been issued a year prior to the female who lived at the residence. The licenses that the officer required her to purchase a year ago had just recently expired.

I arrived at the residence and found it to be in disarray. I observed broken stuff, trash, and a yard not picked up. It was that one stereotypical eyesore of a house on the block. The grass was almost a foot overgrown in the backyard as if it hadn't been mowed for months. The trash can was unmoved and smelled of rotting garbage. This is honestly what I always do first when I get to a house: scan and assess. Take it all in.

I first approached the front door and knocked. Instantly I heard a dog barking inside the house. The dog came to the door, but I could hardly see him through the filthy door window and into the darkness inside the home. All the windows were covered with various items—towels, blankets, anything to provide privacy from anyone seeing inside the home. I then walked around to the back door and knocked on that door as well. Again, more barking but no response from anyone inside. There were no vehicles in the driveway or any indications that anyone was home or tending to the house.

From there, I walked back to my vehicle to pull up expired licenses and see if I could get the owner on the phone. I had a bad feeling about this and wanted to check on these dogs *today*. As I jumped back into my truck, I opened my computer screen, leaned over, and began punching in the address. Within seconds my attention was drawn to some strange feelings on my arms. Glancing down, I couldn't believe what I was seeing. At least fifty fleas covered my uniform, crawling up my pant legs, attacking my arms, and going crazy. I had never in all my years on the job had this experience when simply walking to someone's door to knock. Both the main door and storm doors were closed. The fleas must have been unbelievable in that house. I jumped out of my vehicle instantly, grabbing a can of insect repellent from my truck on my way out. I must have unloaded at least half of the can, dousing my arms and uniform; I pretty much took a bath in it. Any neighbors watching must have been wondering what the hell I was doing and getting a good chuckle if they knew.

Once every inch of me was covered in insect repellent, I got back into my vehicle. The fleas continued to fight through it. I pulled off a big, long piece of heavy-duty tape from the roll I carry with me to post notices and began taping them off my uniform and arms one by one as they jumped on. It was unreal, almost something you would never believe if you didn't see it with your own eyes. By the time I was done, I had a wad of fleas in a ball of tape on the cab floor. Shaking my head in disbelief, I continued investigating the concerns.

I pulled up the previous history and dog license on the computer to get the name of the owner and phone number. I called her several times, but she didn't answer. From there, I walked around to the surrounding neighbors to see if anyone had seen her at the house recently or knew where to find her. I struck out.

No one knew much of anything and hadn't seen her. The neighbor across the street was quite comical. He admitted he was the one that called in the complaint and said he called it in anonymously. "You can't take the risk of people finding out you ratted on them in these parts," he said as he laughed. The neighbor reiterated his concern of not seeing anyone at the house in almost a week and was afraid the dogs were dead inside. I assured him I heard at least one dog barking inside but promised him I would ensure they were alright or take action as soon as possible. He chuckled some more to me about seeing me spraying bug spray all over and probably having a major aroma from it radiating off me. He told me he wished we could crack a Heineken and talk about all the crazy things I see every day. I joked around with him, telling him how he didn't want to know and that I was certain I'd land a write-up from the boss if I had that Heineken with him, especially in my uniform. We laughed and parted ways.

Back to the house, I went. My next step was monitoring the house to see if anyone came in the next twenty-four hours. I can't just go in without a search warrant, a search warrant that proved neglect. I knew that no judge would act on my speculation alone. I pulled out my notices, business cards, and tape. On the two entry doors to the house, I left a notice reading, "Please contact me regarding a complaint that was made. Failure to contact may result in further action taken." Along with the notice, I left my business card taped to the doors. I also taped the doors shut so that I could tell if anyone broke the seal and entered the residence in the next twenty-four hours. Of course, I had to pinch off fifty more fleas after walking to the door to affix the notice and business cards. Over the next day, in between responding to other calls of service, I closely monitored the house and continued to attempt contact with the owner by phone. Nothing changed. This was the additional probable cause I needed to secure a search warrant.

With concerns for the welfare of the animals, the unreal number of fleas pouring out of the residence, the lack of licensing (a misdemeanor offense in my county), the previous history, and the inability to get in contact with the owner, I had to obtain a search warrant to get those dog(s) out of there. That's exactly what I did.

I went back to the office and typed up a search warrant. I carefully detailed what was told to me by neighbors, what I saw, and what this led me to believe. After that was done, I sent it over to the prosecuting attorney and later met with the judge for a signature. This procedure is always a lengthy process, a series of steps that is honestly quite meticulous and time-consuming. I am generally pretty good with tracking people down or getting a hold of them to avoid a search warrant, but this lady was just nowhere to be found. Research found she had no job, no relatives named, rarely came home, had no voicemail to leave a message, nothing. After several hours of my shift went by, I finally had the search warrant in hand. I went to my boss and asked her if she wanted to go on a "field trip." She laughed and asked me what I was getting her into this time. I generally take my supervisor and another officer with me to execute a search warrant, for safety reasons and just to have other witnesses for court purposes.

With the number of fleas I expected to be walking into, I grabbed a couple of Tyvek body suits with hoods and boot covers, preparing for the worst. Those are the white hazmat-type suits that zip up. I called in another officer to meet me and my boss. He, too, responded with, "What now?" I have a reputation in my department for finding some of the worst situations involving animals. They all think I am a magnet for animal cruelty and neglect. Once we were all together and prepared, we headed out to the house and met up with the local police, who generally stand by for safety reasons as well.

We all arrived at the residence and positioned ourselves by the roles we served. Police are standing by outside, myself to knock, announce, and enter, my partner right behind me to protect me from dog aggression, and my boss ready to make judgment calls. The neighbors, especially the complainant, were surely peering out their windows and going "holy crap; she wasn't kidding when she said she would handle it."

I anticipated walking into a house full of fleas with a dog or two that weren't in adequate condition, and not licensed—somewhat of a routine neglection concern. I hoped not to be walking in to find one dog alive and another dead.

My partner and I approached the door, covered in flea spray. I warned the whole team about the fleas. I knocked on the door in an authoritative manner several times, calling out, "Animal control, we have a search warrant."

No response. After several minutes of no response to the announcements, we broke into the residence to secure the dog(s). The first dog that greeted us at the door was a German shepherd mix. That dog was the dominant, "You're not coming in here," kind of dog. She was just doing what dogs are expected to do, threatening to attack when we came in. Once on a dog snare and allowed outside, she realized we were friendly and only there to help. The second dog that greeted us at the door was also a shepherd-type mixed breed and a male. I was so relieved they both greeted us, and one wouldn't be found dead in the house somewhere. He allowed me to put a leash on him and pull him out. They were both scratching excessively and showed signs of extreme flea infestations. They were missing hair on their back ends, indicative of flea dermatitis. Flea dermatitis is when the animal with fleas experiences itching and hair loss around the base of the tail, which results in scabs and crusty skin. We quickly loaded them in the vehicle to secure them, planning an exam upon impoundment to the shelter once the search for any other animals was completed.

• • •

We stepped into our Tyvek suits for protection and, knowing the dogs were secure, my partner and I entered the residence together. We had to check for any more animals. I took a couple of steps into the residence with my boss standing outside the door and stepped right back out. I needed a minute to process what I had just seen and, of course, swear a few times.

"Holy, ****," I said to my boss about how unreal the situation inside was. I have been doing this job for years, and the conditions I saw in this home immediately made my top ten list. There was feces *everywhere*. When I say feces *everywhere*, I mean feces *everywhere*. It was deplorable! There had to have been a couple *hundred* piles of feces in the dining room area alone. The feces were in various stages of molding and decomposing. After walking through the house and finding no more animals, I photographed the scene. I discovered the basement *full of feces* as well. I found hundreds more piles of feces there. Altogether, there were well over a thousand piles of feces in that house, probably two thousand. It was like the place was covered in *a feces carpet*.

There were no words for how disgusting that house was. I didn't find any food or water for the dogs, but the owner must have been coming to care for them at intervals because the dogs didn't show any indications of being severely underweight. After I verified there were no other animals in the house, photographed the scene, and left my search warrant, we called the code enforcement department over to secure the door. They tagged the house as inhabitable, as expected. The code enforcement officer begged me to take his camera in the house and take photos, so he didn't have to enter. It was *that* bad. The police wouldn't even cross the street curb they were so disgusted by the number of fleas and conditions said to be inside. I didn't blame them. There was no excuse for this. It doesn't take money or anything more than bending over and shoveling all the feces outside to clean this up. This was pure neglect and laziness. Inexcusable.

Back at the shelter, I pulled the dogs out one at a time so the veterinarian could photograph and assess them. The extent of the injuries on the dogs was worse than we thought. Fleas covered every part of their bodies. Their hair was crunchy to the touch with a layer of flea dirt, black specks of a dirt-like substance on the skin near the base of the hair. A wipe of their bodies with a wet rag left the rag red from the blood the fleas were sucking out. At the base of one dog's tail, I counted over five hundred fleas in just a small area.

The veterinarian found the dogs to be anemic from all the fleas, meaning the fleas were slowly sucking so much blood out of the dogs, they were weakened and heading towards death as a result. These poor dogs' condition was sickening. The dogs were treated with rapid-acting flea-killing pills as well as flea preventative. We had to house them in an isolated area of the shelter so as not to allow any other animals exposure to the unreal amount of fleas they contained.

A couple of days later, the owner called. She had gone to the house and discovered the notices, business cards, and search warrant. Of course, she had also found that the dogs were no longer there. I welcomed her to come to the shelter and discuss the situation. She did.

The interview lasted less than ten minutes. I didn't have much to say other than there was no excuse for the conditions of her dogs and that I would be pursuing a warrant for her arrest. She tried to give me a sob story about this and that going on in her life, but I kept bringing up the fact that if she had lifted up a shovel in her home (I did see one on the property) and scraped some feces out, making an *effort* to care for her dogs, I would maybe be interested in hearing her excuses. She knew she was wrong and didn't argue it. She surrendered ownership of her dogs on the spot and didn't refute anything further. I told her to expect a warrant out for her arrest and explained the rest would be up to the courts. I wasn't disrespectful or rude, I was just brutally honest, as you must be in this job.

After typing up the report, documenting the veterinarian's finding, and attaching the photos as evidence, within days I had a warrant out for her arrest. She again wouldn't answer her phone (the one she called me on, the one I tried calling originally) and wouldn't show her face to anyone. For quite some time, she continued to evade law enforcement. One day. I got word that the media did a story on her house. I pulled the story up online. The neighbors apparently had all been calling the city police department and code enforcement offices because the fleas began invading their surrounding homes after I removed the dogs (the fleas' food source).

The neighboring animals had to be treated for fleas, and even the local residents were being bitten by fleas. Unreal. The city code compliance department couldn't get ahold of the homeowner/dog owner to hold her responsible. The police department called me, hoping to get her arrested, but I, too, had been unable to find her. The reporter walked up to the dog owner's door while his crew was filming and knocked to show that no one would come to the door. Shortly after knocking, you hear him start panicking and jumping. It had taken him just a few moments to discover scores of fleas crawling up his pants and all over his body. I laughed over and over at this. I felt his pain. *Been there done that.* Within a day of the media airing the story, tips flooded in, and the suspect was arrested by the local police department on an animal neglect warrant.

It was a happy ending for these dogs. After days of flea treatments and constant care, the dogs pulled through their anemia and were taken in by a local rescue organization for their pursuit of a suitable and loving home. It was a relief to get those animals out of that horrible situation, and I was proud of myself for getting the job done.

CHAPTER EIGHTEEN

Xena

It was the middle of summer, and the calls coming into dispatch were at an all-time high rate. Usually, it was just one dispatcher sitting in the small office at the shelter, picking up one call after the next, even having to put a call on hold to finish up the one prior. The dispatcher would have to jot down all the relevant information of the complaint, time stamp it, and radio an officer the information. It wasn't uncommon to see the dispatcher holding the phone on a shoulder, writing with one hand, using the other to hold the radio mic to communicate back and forth with some of the six officers on the road at a time, hearing their arrival call, clear the call, or to check a license. Summer months are always extremely fast-paced, trying to keep up with all the pending complaints. Summer is a time when everyone is outside mingling, and the kids are off school.

Dogs accidentally get out the door and attack other dogs or people. People have their windows open, and dogs break through screens and then jump out of the windows. People are outside, hearing and seeing concerns with animals, so they are calling those in. The list goes on.

On this particular day in June, the local city police department called in a concern about a dog at an address in the city. The address was in a well-known drug neighborhood. The police had actually left a message on our anonymous tip line voicemail with their concern since they were at the house in the middle of the night on something unrelated. All the police officer said in the voicemail was to please check on the dog at that address because they noticed "something wrong" with the dog's muzzle when they were there last night.

Originally, another animal control officer was sent. Sometimes in the summer, if I was too backed up with investigations, dispatch would send the other officers to the initial complaint to see if it was something they could handle without needing an investigation. The notes in the computer by that officer said he didn't have any contact with anyone when he went to the house. The neighbors told him they thought the occupants were taken to jail by the police who had been seen at the residence the night before. The animal control officer left a notice posted on the front door asking whoever lived there to call. After no response, he went back the next day. The notice he left was removed. He posted a second notice to firm up his request to contact.

Meanwhile, that same day, the local humane society

called dispatch to make a complaint about a concern they had. The humane society worker told our dispatcher they had someone walk in and drop off a dog claiming it was a "stray," and that it had a concerning mark around its muzzle. Their veterinarian on staff examined the dog and said it appeared the marks were from the dog's mouth being tied shut for an extended period. Around the same time, a person unwilling to identify themselves to dispatch, called about the second notice posted on the door. The caller told our dispatcher there was no longer a dog at the house.

That was when the officer called me directly on the phone and said, "I think this one needs some in-depth investigation."

To me, something wasn't right with this one. To add confusion, the person that turned the dog in to the humane society, which was in the neighboring county, claimed they found the dog in that county. The neighboring county had also opened an investigation. This is another responsibility of the dispatcher, an important one at that: putting together information and noticing when things are related.

When I got this case, the first thing I knew was that the dog was safe at the humane society. That meant I wasn't in a huge rush. In a lot of cases, you're racing the clock to solve the case because you want to get the animal out of the situation. I started my investigation by typing up a quick email to the local police department requesting the body camera footage and their police report from the night they were at this house. I wanted to start at the beginning to see exactly what had transpired that night.

Meanwhile, while I waited for a response, I went back to the house and knocked myself. I'm not sure if it's that I'm a female and don't look very intimidating or what, but I often have much better success getting people to answer their doors and engage with me than the other (male) officers do. It was now five days since the police originally called in this concern. When I pulled up to the house, I looked around and saw a typical city house that, quite honestly, looked like a crack house. The lawn was mowed but not with care. The blinds were drawn or blankets were covering the windows. A pathway had been beaten through the grass to the door by frequent foot traffic—all the buyers rushing in and out, buying drugs I suspect.

I approached the door and knocked, always standing off-center from the door in case a bullet was to fly through. I always casually put my boot against the door in case a dog charges the storm door (at me) when the main door is open. Trust me, it happens way more than you'd believe.

After knocking, I was surprised when a woman opened the door. She looked to be in her mid-thirties, skinny, and not fully dressed. She spoke softly and slowly, displaying the overall appearance of a crack or meth addict. It was her look of blankness, like you could tell there's not much emotion, just a vacant look in her eye, like, "My only worry is where my next hit gonna come from." I'll call her Jane for the purpose of this story.

Jane and I talked for a minute, me on the front porch, her with the door cracked open, standing inside. I told her who I was and why I was there. I always approach everyone with a calm, personable demeanor. I'm never rude or treat people like they are less than me. I honestly despise law enforcement officers who act like that. There is, of course, a place and time to get pushy or authoritative, but the conversation should never start out like that unless it's warranted.

Jane and I talked back and forth for quite a while. She told me she was the "aid" for a person in the house who is bedridden due to a spinal injury. Jane claimed she had been coming to the house for several weeks but doesn't actually live here. She's just here all the time. This is a common story of crack and meth users. They frequent the house where the crack/meth is, always wanting to make sure they are where the next fix is. Jane told me in addition to her and Dennis, the bedridden tenant, there was a guy named Cory staying at the house as well, but he wasn't there now.

Cory, Jane said, had a dog named "Xena," and one of "Xena's" puppies lived there too. Jane went on to tell me Xena was a white pit bull mix. Jane made it a point to tell me that Xena was very afraid of Cory, describing how Xena would pancake on the ground in fear when Cory would come around. Jane said she honestly rarely saw Cory. When he was there, he would always be in the basement where the dogs always were. I told Jane that I had concerns about Xena's muzzle, and she nodded her head confirming. Jane said she remembered asking Cory about it a week or so earlier when she noticed it. Cory first told her to mind her own business; that Xena is his dog, and he'll do what he wants. Later, Jane said, Cory claimed

Xena got off her chain and hurt her snout running loose. Jane admitted she didn't believe that.

Jane said Cory went to jail the day the police were there and remained there still. According to Jane, Cory also had a girlfriend, and the girlfriend took Xena to the humane society and the puppy to a farmhouse that wanted it. This conversation with Jane was excellent for my investigation. I had a statement identifying Cory as the owner of the dog, which was, in fact, the dog from the humane society.

After some rapport-building back-and-forth conversation on the front porch, Jane let her guard down when she felt I didn't pose any threat to her or her crack. Jane welcomed me into the house to talk with the tenant, who, she said, was bedridden due to his spinal injury from falling off a ladder. As I stepped in, I gazed around, seeing a typical crack house. There was next to no furniture, and a crack house smell lingered in the air. It was the smell of druggies smoking cigarettes, hanging at the house for days on end without showering, waiting for their next fix. It was a stale, dark, shut-up house smell.

Jane led me to a bedroom just off the living room on the main level. I stood in the doorway, respectfully introducing myself to a guy lying in bed in a brace and clearly pretty messed up from his spinal injury. The guy reiterated what Jane said, and even told me a few things he'd heard that sounded like Cory abusing Xena in the basement when he was there. I thanked them both for their time, collected their names and phone numbers, and left them with my business card for now.

Meanwhile, I received my police report back with the body camera footage. The footage showed the police rip-roaring into the house in the middle of the night and taking Cory to jail after he was acting like an idiot, ripping up the front yard by spinning his tires because he was feuding with someone else. Cory had methamphetamine on him when arrested, confirming my suspicions of the house. The body camera footage showed the police walking through the house and talking to other meth addicts while they dealt with the situation. The police shined the flashlight down the basement stairs in the house, and there was Xena at the bottom of the steps, scared to come upstairs, barking at the officer in fear. The officer made a comment to another officer about how she was going to call animal control to check on that dog down there because it "Sure had a weird mark around its muzzle" as they proceeded with their police business. This officer was the one who left that message on our tip line that night—what a great officer she was for taking that extra minute out of her day to do that. Some of the officers don't advocate for animals as she did.

Using my computer resources, I found Cory in jail about an hour away. It looked like he had a warrant out of that county, so he was transferred there after dealing with his charges here locally. I called up the neighboring county animal control officer, who had also opened an investigation on this case and gave her an update on my findings so far. We were fairly certain this would solely be a case in my jurisdiction (county), but she offered to accompany me up to the jail to interview Cory anyway. We coordinated our schedules for the next day. I was determined to keep him in jail, and only got more motivated with each new piece of evidence that would help land him there.

At this point, it had been about eight days since I began the investigation. I was chipping away at the case little by little each day the best I could between all my other cases. The other officer and I arrived at the jail. They set us up in an interview room and left to go get Cory. Cory walked in with his chest puffed out and a chip on his shoulder. The other officer and I introduced ourselves, and I proceeded to read him his Miranda Rights. This is always a requirement if someone is in custody. I told Cory we were there about Xena to address some concerns we were trying to get resolved.

Cory began talking as if he was some hero, saying how he got Xena from some lady that wasn't feeding her when her son went to prison. Cory admitted that he was living in the basement of that crack house, hiding out from the police for weeks because he was on the run from warrants. Cory talked about his girlfriend "Dani," who had Xena a lot, and Xena's puppy, that was also at the house. Continuing, Cory complained about the five to six people always at the house when he was there. He said he hated the occasional drug raids.

The interview switched gears. I brought up Xena's face, saying that we are investigating what happened to her. Cory first claimed he didn't know, telling us a story about Xena getting loose for a couple of hours and coming back that way.

He surmised it was probably a raccoon that had rearranged Xena's muzzle.

As we talked more, Cory told us a different story. When it was brought up that his stories were differing, he became defensive, puffing up his chest further. "You're going to believe all those Heroin junkies in that house?"

"Like I did something to that mother fucking dog," Cory continued his unhelpful monologue, probably using bullying tactics that worked in the past with other people. He became hostile and threatened us, hoping we would get scared and back down. In a rage, Cory went on and on about how he put peroxide on Xena's face and blessed that dog, blah blah blah. Then his rage escalated, with him saying, "I don't give a fuck about that dog. No, I give ZERO fucks about that dog." We were getting nowhere with our questioning or the conversation. Cory was one angry individual who had some clear anger issues. He had difficulties controlling himself, that was for sure. I determined that, due to his methamphetamine addiction, he wasn't going to tell us the truth. When we brought up the subject of Xena's muzzle wound, Cory became enraged.

It wasn't worth it to me to keep pressing when I knew his type. Applying more pressure wouldn't get me a confession. I had what I needed for the day. Cory admitted owning the dog. He admitted she had injuries to her face, and he never took her for medical care. Now I just had to find out what he really did to that dog.

I next tracked down Cory's now ex-girlfriend Dani's mother. The mother told me how she's known Cory for many, many years because of her daughter. She said Cory was a scary, abusive guy. The mother said she was pretty sure Cory suffered from some sort of bipolar disorder. Dani's mother told me that Cory used to punch Xena to gain control over Dani. Dani even told her mother that Xena had a black eye the week before because Cory had tied her mouth shut. The mother said she heard a rumor that Cory tied Xena's mouth shut with duct tape, but she really wasn't sure. The mother gave me the name of another girl who might know the truth, saying that girl was her other son's—Dani's brother—friend. Dani's mother went on to say how Cory was always threatening their family—her, her daughter, and her other children. The mother agreed to give me her son's contact information so I could talk to him.

I called up Dani's brother, Mark, and talked to him on the phone. Mark went on and on about what a terrible person Cory was, saying that Cory had severe mental issues which made him dangerously angry at times. Mark said that when Cory got angry, it was like he just had to beat up a person, and when he couldn't, he would beat up an animal. Mark told me how Cory had been on the run from the police for a long time and how he's been using his brother's identity, and that's how he evades the police so often.

Mark told me he'd been around Cory a few times at that house, saying when Xena would get up wagging her tail to greet someone walking in, he would yell at her "Go lay the fuck down!" He also remembered Cory slapping

Xena on the face. Mark told me how much he hated Cory. He talked about how Cory would be abusive to his sister, and when his sister finally recently left him, Cory threatened his whole family, telling them to "Consider themselves in pine boxes."

Next, I talked to Dani. She was a typical domestic violence victim. She didn't want to say much but did tell me about Xena, and how Cory got her. Dani told me she broke off her relationship with Cory about a month prior and hadn't seen Xena much since. Dani admitted while they were dating, there were quite a few incidents when Cory would do "mean stuff" to Xena. When pressed, Dani told me about a time when Cory beat Xena so badly she hid in the bathtub with the curtain drawn and wouldn't come out, but stayed shaking and pancaked in the tub. Dani began crying, saying she could never intervene out of fear Cory would come after her.

She did admit Cory would use Xena as leverage to get to her. There was one day Dani remembered when she tried to break things off with Cory. He called her and told her she had one hour to come, or he was going to kill Xena. Dani told me she heard from a friend that Cory put duct tape around Xena's face, but that I should talk to a woman named "Pam", who frequents that house, for more information. Dani admitted she was the one who took Xena to the humane society the day after animal control left the note on the door of that house. She said someone from the house called her and told her to take care of the dog. Dani pleaded with me to make sure Cory never had an animal again.

It had now been ten days since the call was placed to us to check on this dog. My investigation was moving forward little by little, but I still needed to prove beyond a reasonable doubt what this guy did to Xena's face and what he used to do it. I needed a witness or some solid evidence. With everything I knew now, I circled back to the beginning and went back to the house—the crime scene.

Jane answered the door again, allowing me in. This time, Jane provided more information. She first directed me to a basement trash bag where I found Xena's collar with a tag. Jane came out and told me her friend, Janie, was visiting the house and saw Cory tie electrical tape around Xena's muzzle. She remembered Janie running up from downstairs crying and upset that day, saying Cory put electrical tape on Xena's mouth. Jane claimed she misunderstood Janie, not realizing Cory had left it on, saying she would have done something if she had known that. Jane just remembered Janie being very upset about what happened and leaving the house.

I went to the Humane Society where Xena was being housed as evidence to this case. The Humane Society gave me their veterinarian's write-up and evaluation, as well as photos of her when she first came in. The cause of the injury was noted to be a rope, leash, or tape wrapped around her face for an extended period of time—likely a couple of days with her face swelling up from the tightness of the tape and causing circulation loss. I couldn't leave just yet, I had to meet this dog. They took me back and got her out of her cage. She was the sweetest. Even to me, in my big scary uniform and shiny boots and badge, she wagged her tail at my presence and had no clue how terribly heartbreaking her face looked with a giant circular scab healing around it. I thanked the staff for all they had been doing for her. I promised I was doing everything I possibly could to get Cory behind bars for this.

I won't forget the next phone call. I was off duty, driving out on the country roads and heading over to my mother's house for something after work. I almost never carry my work phone with me. I have this rule of thumb in order to avoid burnout—I need *me time*, too. When I'm off duty, I need to be fully off duty. There were, however, some cases for which I made exceptions. This was one of them. My work phone rang as I was driving down the road. I listened to the voicemail after missing the call and realized it was Janie. Jane had given her my number as I begged her to, and she called! This might become my smoking gun on this case. I quickly pulled my car off the road at a roadside power station and called her back. Waiting for her to answer, I was frantically digging for a pen and paper in my car. I introduced myself to Janie and eased into the conversation. Janie told me how she was at Cory's in the basement with him and another guy that night. She remembered Xena and a little white puppy being down there too.

Janie remembered Cory getting really mad at Xena (the "mom dog," as she described her) because the puppy had peed on the couch. Janie told me she remembered Cory grabbing the mom dog and began beating her head against the wall. Janie tried to intervene but was too scared. She was crying on the phone to me, telling me how she wanted to stop it, but "He was just way bigger than me" and really could have come after her. Janie went on to say, while sobbing, he took the mom dog and taped her mouth shut with electrical tape that he grabbed off the work area near the pool table. Janie said Cory was kicking the mom dog while doing this.

As she continued sobbing, Janie described how Cory roughly threw the mom dog with her mouth taped shut and the puppy in a wire crate in the basement near the washing machine. She said Cory proceeded to take the hose off the washer and turn on the water, and spray the two dogs in the cage. She said he did it "over and over." That's when Janie ran up the stairs, bawling her eyes out, and ran out of the house. Janie told me it was one of the worst things she had ever seen in her life.

The next day, I returned to that house one final time. I had a signed consent to search the house and I went through that basement with a fine-tooth comb. While searching the basement, I remembered people coming in and out. I'm sure they were there to buy crack, but that wasn't my concern—I wanted to put this guy away for animal abuse. In a pile of garbage near the basement stairs, I found the tape! It was my final missing piece of evidence. My case was rock solid. Not only was the tape in the shape of Xena's muzzle but on the sticky side, it was covered in her tiny little nose hairs that ripped off when the tape was removed.

I took the tape to the crime lab for analysis. The lab could confirm that it was dog hair, that the hair matched that dog, how many hairs they found, and how that would be consistent with it being wrapped around the dog's muzzle.

I turned in my report to the prosecutor's office, which drafted a felony animal cruelty arrest warrant for Cory without question. Since he was already sitting in jail, this new charge would just stack on top of those he was already facing.

Truthfully, I'm not sure where Xena ended up. I didn't really worry about it with that particular Humane Society. They were great people and wouldn't allow anything but royal treatment for that dog after what she went through—I'm sure of it. My role was just to give them a call to let them know they were free to adopt her out and no longer needed to hold her as evidence, as the court told me. I wasn't even called to court for this case, which is not uncommon when you leave no stone unturned in your investigation, when nothing is refutable. I did, however, hear a rumor that the judge ripped him a new one in the courtroom during sentencing. Well-done, judge!